Selling Security

Reactive Based Service To Proactive Marketing & Sales

Bill Wise CPP
Joey Dalessio

With Illustrations By
Danny deBruin

"It is not the strongest of the species that survive, nor the most intelligent, but the one most responsive to change".

Charles Darwin

The information and recommendations in this book are necessarily general in nature and do not guarantee results. The actions and recommendations we describe are considered common security business marketing practices that can be beneficial in creating an effective sales and marketing program. However, no book or program can guarantee results.

By purchasing this book, the buyer agrees to the above disclaimer. Those purchasing this book may use the procedures, practices, examples and illustrations found in this book for their own internal company use only.

© 2008 Security Wise Group LLC®
http://www.securitywisegroup.com

ISBN: 978-0-6151-8602-3

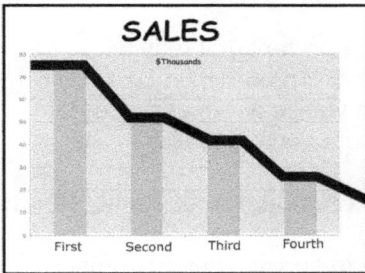

Meet Daryl. He owns AAA Security Services and discovers one day that because of new competition, his sales are off the chart. But in the wrong direction!

Table of Contents:

Get more "face time" with your existing customers.
After Your Marketing Event – Now What?
Learn how to follow up on what you have learned from your customers.
Use your customer face time to trigger sales proposals.
Survey attendees and learn how to make the event even better next time!

Keep Your Customers With Newsletters And E-mail Programs

Find out why newsletter programs can help you retain your customers.
Educate your customers on new products and services.
Inform your customers about current crime trends in your community and show them how they can reduce their exposure!
Grab new customers With Direct Mail
What is the best type of direct mail?
Learn about mailing lists
What should you expect as a return on your investment?
How do you measure success?

Build Relationships That Last

Beyond the newsletter!
Learn about some of the things that you can do to create a long-term Business Partnership.
Learn about what the academic experts say about Relationship Marketing.
And More!

Part II   **Implementing Change & Deciding To Take Action**

Transitioning To Proactive Marketing

Special: How To Build A Successful Company!
Planning for change.
Highly focused marketing and selling!
Developing the plan.

Deciding what functions you need to operate!
Identifying accountabilities - Who is responsible?
You need SMART Planning!
And More!

Creating a plan & create a job description.
What should the employment ad say to capture the best candidates?
Identifying key position attributes to guarantee plan success!
Interview questions to sort out "good, better and best" hires.
Does your business environment support the plan?
Learn about Your Leadership Behavior!
You must do a background check!
Joey D's Lessons Learned!

Set up a written training plan!
Measure learning using quizzes and practical exercises.
What about using source books and materials?
Joey D's Lessons From Successes - Training

You've done the planning, put it in writing, budgeted the funds and rolled out the program.
Learn how to measure your success.
How you can analyze your company performance and put your best assets into overdrive!

.

Call to ACTION!
What we hoped that you learned.
Learn about us and where to find resources to help you plan and succeed!
Find out about forms and tools that we have available and seminars to learn more.

Daryl knows that there are some things he needs to change at AAA Security!

Introduction

The art and science of marketing your security hardware, equipment and systems to residential and commercial end user customers has experienced a startling change in recent years. We think it has been at least at the same pace as other developments in communications technology have occurred. Your younger customers have embraced the technological changes instantly while your older established customers may be struggling with understanding how change will impact what they know has worked for them in the past.

Future trends are impossible to guess even though many are obvious. For instance, we are clearly leaving behind mechanical locks with metal keys. When was the last time you checked into a hotel and the clerk gave you a metal room key with a plastic tag? Virtually all hotels use electronic locks with programmable plastic cards. How long will car manufacturers continue to use mechanical locks? Owners of GM cars need only call "OnStar" to have an electronic signal sent to the car in the event of a lockout. All of you BMW owners get E-mails generated by your car when it is time for routine service. On the other hand, back in the 50's and 60's they told us that we would all be flying around town in our own private aircraft like the cartoon "Jetsons".

The trend toward electronic hardware integration is not without controversy. In many cases, an electronic lock may not mean better security for an organization especially if there is a keyed lock cylinder over ride. As with all security components and schemes, the greatest vulnerability to failure lies with the people who manage the system. Poor controls and lack of clear security policies and procedures will eventually doom the most sophisticated hardware system to irrelevancy.

This book can't predict what changes will occur in your products and your business in the future or the best way to deal with how those transitional changes will impact the results of all of your hard work! For that reason, we have included a lot of information that you can use for your sales program initiatives that deals with building trusted business relationships with your existing customers. And we introduce you to programs that will help you to ask the right questions and that will to allow you to create proposals offering your customers business solution programs rather than just selling a lock or alarm service.

By selling comprehensive prevention solutions to your customers you're selling a process or methodology by which your customers adopt a systems approach to preventing a negative experience that impacts the business profitability. The system that you sell has to include how your hardware products will integrate into the customers business, affect the people using it and provide positive impact by including a process to manage the hardware products that provide a barrier to the loss of assets.

Can you use a marketing book to make more sales and profit for your business? We say that you can by using what you learn here to create a Marketing Roadmap that you can use to guide you through a goal setting and action planning process, on to budgeting resources, program rollout and tracking success on your P&L.

Transitioning from a reactive operations based business to proactive sales and marketing needs a plan! Your Roadmap Plan should be a bridge using your sales goals and marketing initiatives that can be "benchmarked" to measure progress and success. This book will tell you about a number of transition strategies you can use and how they have worked for other companies like yours!

The key to this book can be found in the pages of Part II, which describes in detail how to go about creating a supportive environment for the development of a sales and marketing function in your business. We believe that until you get serious about developing this function within your company, many of you will continue to depend on the phone ringing to bring in business and are likely to watch while sales growth and success goes to your competitors who have the vision to move forward using sales and marketing methodology.

The creation of a professional sales and marketing function is within your grasp and we will show you how to select, train and develop marketing people to go after the business that is most profitable to your organization.

Your security product and service business can take a quantum leap into a higher level of recognition by becoming the premier services integration company in your marketplace.

While we have written this book for the security hardware business owner including both locksmith based and the alarm based operators, there is really no reason why any service related business couldn't profit from the information you will find.

Bill Wise CPP & Joey Dalessio

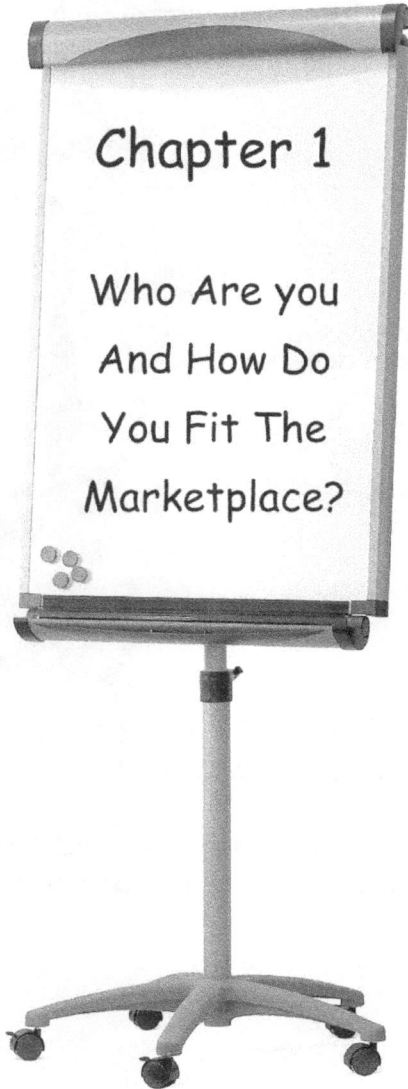

Chapter 1

Who Are you
And How Do
You Fit The
Marketplace?

**Daryl discovers why
his prices keep going up!**

Rising international demand for commodities
and a weakening dollar is driving prices up.

Three bucks a gallon for gas and supply prices
doubling, AAA Security is fast becoming a Non-Profit!

**Chapter 1   Who Are You and How Do You Fit Into
                        Your Marketplace?**

What are the services you provide? Is your primary business Locksmith-ing? What about Alarms and CCTV Cameras systems? Do you provide some services but not others? For instance, we find many locksmith-based businesses do not deal in integrated access control systems or alarms. Conversely, many alarm-based companies seem very comfortable with all things electrical such as cameras, alarms and access controls but refrain from dealing with locks and safes. Do you consider your company as pro-viding security systems integration?

Joey D's Lessons Learned – An Early Lesson

The Security Business of today is not your Father's Lock Shop! Market-ing 101 in the current business environment begins with image; people see orange and think building products or yellow arches and taste burgers and fries. The "association" of these businesses is firmly planted in our mind. When someone sees your vehicles or store what do they see? Do they see what you hope is your vision of your brand?

Do they look at your store-front and think "fix-it" shop, key or lock shop or Se-curity Store? Do they see images of keys and padlocks or closed cir-cuit television cameras and keypads? Consum-ers think differently than technicians and techni-cians think differently from business owners. How far removed from the custom-er is your thinking?

Do your vehicles resem-ble Sanford and Son or are they professionally and art-fully done? Are they clean, do they look in disre-pair? Is the signage tired? Are the shelves orderly? These seemingly com-

Over on 2nd Ave. Joe waits for a customer

mon sense questions reflect the far too common image people have of the "lock and key" business as a "fix-it second hand shop by a very busy storekeeper.

How do you begin changing the image, and building your brand? Want to have an awakening? Park across the street from your building and observe for an hour or so, or drive by as a passenger in the back seat and observe from every angle or direction a customer to your place of business might view. What will they see? Are the windows sparkling? Are there eye-catching displays? Is the lighting sufficient? Does your business have "curb appeal" or are there signs blocking the windows? Does your door and adjacent side panel glass resemble a neighborhood bulletin board for local merchants? You know, guitar lessons, yoga class signs, house painting services and bikes fixed too?

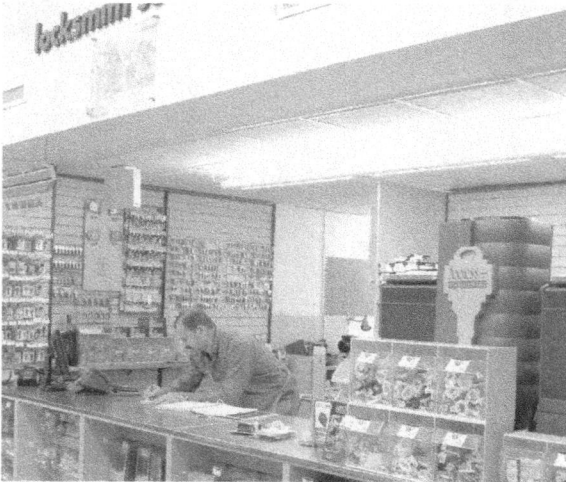

Let's walk inside your store. What will your customer and what will we see? What can we feel? What will we hear? Today consumers want to see and feel. It is amazing that we are in a high tech security business product world but the decisions to buy are made by our customers who not only want to see the product but also have to be able to touch and feel?

That is why you have to remember to have displays that operate interactively. Is there anything worse for sales than a product on display that does not work? How about do you have "story boards" to tell about the product and how it operates? Have you thought to maybe even go over the top with a passive infrared motion detector that trips a signal to begin audio on demand instruction? Finally, does the display include manufacturers up to date advertising collateral? Has their experience in your store prompted them to buy the item NOW?

It is amazing how showrooms can become wall and shelf storage facilities for free display boards and mounts. It is even more amazing how retail counter space is eaten up by more and more trinkets and impulse buying items that take up very valuable retail space. Would you know what you were looking at if you were the consumer? Do you really make enough money from cartoon character key tags to devote all of your front area display space to multiple racks of the stuff? Space that could be used for high end and high profit security hardware products?

For example padlock display boards either show actual sizes or have one sample and an outline of the various sizes available. Does the board really provide information on how to select the right padlock?

Why not a "story board" that identifies what attributes are available and the benefits of each, and let the consumer identify the ones that serve their real or perceived needs or that provides a platform for the professional to inform then recommend the right padlock.

Features like resistance to cutting by hacksaws, or resistant to attack by bolt cutters, or cutting wheels, to a degree that is reasonable for the cost of the padlock and what it is protecting. Today consumers are looking for padlocks that resist picking and bumping, shimmying or general vandalism and all padlocks are not created equal!

It is even likely people would like to prevent unauthorized key duplication, given an opportunity to make the choice. People do not inherently know what is available, and they seldom can tell from a wall or rack display. Move the game up a notch in your store!

There are many business models that exist to provide security services and hardware to end user companies and the general public homeowner marketplace, as it exists today. The history of many security companies began with a single discipline. In the case of the locksmith trade, it can be said that the beginning was a trade guild environment, which required many years of practice to learn how to construct the locks and barriers needed to protect valuables. The evolution of the industrial use of electricity to run motors and electric powered mechanical devices brought us into the age of the first burglar alarms in local banks.

What about the services you don't provide that your competitors do? If you are not involved in access control, do you think that mechanical locks will be around forever? How about fire alarm systems? Do you provide consulting services offering your customers loss prevention policies and procedures to govern the operations of the electronic and mechanical security systems that you sell?

What ever your current role happens to be today, it is clear that it is all about to change for the business operator who considers themselves a specialist. If you are the owner of a company with a very narrow list of specialized services, fasten your seatbelt because you may be in for a wild ride!

What are some of the business model list of paradigms in the industry? We present the following information without any intention of making any negative judgments about a particular business model. A business with low overhead and minimal numbers of employees can be startlingly profitable.

The first category that we see, we like to call "Service Based". This business model is what many see as the historical model of the locksmith and basic alarm installation trades. This production-oriented practitioner is dependent upon reacting to phone orders or walk-in customer traffic. The order taker is often found working out of a small shop, kiosk or even out of a service truck. Almost all of his advertising can be spent on a primary position in the local yellow pages. Which often figures into the selection of his company name.

The company name, by the way, often starts with multiples of the letter "A" to achieve a high position among the yellow book listings ahead of his competitors. The remaining marketing budget is spent on pens, pencils and occasional community newspaper ads. His business is entirely production oriented, responsive and incident driven. Depending on the market, this model can also expand into a much larger organization with several trucks on the road running from call to call trying to keep up with service demands. That is, if the area population is on the increase with subsequent demand increases and competition does not.

So, our definition of production oriented, means that he spends little time on sales efforts to find new business and in some cases his paucity of record keeping prevents him from establishing a meaningful plan to service and retain his existing customer base. He responds to the phone call for service from customers both old and new and can be very busy. He knows that the yellow book ads do work for many people because that is where they look to find him when they are locked out of their cars or their businesses or homes and need his services.

He is a worker bee, and we know many of these folks that practice this basic model and do very well financially. These folks often tell us that they are so busy that they cannot consider doing any other tasks even if it means more business for their company. Right now they have all the work that they can possibly handle!

This business model is also highly vulnerable to competition in the form of a competitor that uses marketing techniques to inform the customer that they are more cost effective and readily available to take care of a broad range of security systems issues that the business owner has. They don't wait for the phone to ring; professional appearing and knowledgeable sales people are on the phone targeting their ideal customer profile, they visit the business and describe the equipment and services that are available at competitive prices. They follow up with marketing collateral and phone calls that reminds the business owner who to call and why.

The next category is similar to the first paradigm but with a few key differences. We'll call him the "The CML Pro". The primary difference is that the technical expertise is significantly more advanced and these guys often achieve professional trade certifications (like Certified Master Locksmith!). Since the list of things that they can fix includes some electrical hardware such as electronic safes, stand-alone electronic locks and camera systems, they are often the provider of choice for small businesses getting started with electronics. They call the "Pro" because they know him from all the years that he fixed their mechanical door locks.

Another new thing about the Pro is that he will often notice security hardware that he can improve on when he visits his customers and will make recommendations when he speaks with the business owner. So by being more proactive he finds ways to increase his sales by finding more things to do during the visit. The Pro is also often extremely busy and is so stretched he will tell you that he simply has no time to invest in adding marketing programs to his business!

The best of these practitioners, however, are in the process of shifting their

business model from reactive to proactive. They recognize that there are significant advantages to directing their labor and capital toward activities that return the greatest profit margin to their company bottom line. So they make a point of telling their customers about the advantages of switching to new technologies. They start expanding and advertising their service and product offerings and do a lot more selling at every opportunity. The less profitable tasks more and more become back burner fill in for the available time that occurs during a lull in the high profit jobs.

Joey D's Lessons from Successes - From Reactive Problem Solver to Proactive Solution Sales

Artery Lock Service, Inc.
Medford, MA

The transition from yesteryear to the present day while planning for the future is a challenge many companies have overcome. In the locksmith business the first transition is from a reactive service based company to a proactive solutions sales based mechanical lock business. This has been accomplished through the marketing and selling of patented key control products.

The impact of focus is really in the numbers. The reactive service company has no idea who will call on the telephone or visit the business next. You need technicians skilled in multiple areas, a wide inventory and tools and knowledge over a wide spectrum. As the business owner, with all that investment, you hope people will know to visit you, but hope is not a reliable strategy and in fact it is reactive and could be a deadly strategy today.

Artery Lock Service, Inc. has an outstanding reputation as a family owned lock and security business with a hands-on owner since 1960. When key control products first arrived on the market in the early seventies, Artery Lock Service was one of the pioneers in the Greater Boston, Massachusetts area, selling patented key control systems to local municipalities, condo's, apartments and local businesses. The effort to do so was typically influenced by theft of some type with the owner or manager looking for a solution. This was an "active" posture in lieu of reactive in that customers did not ask for a solution by product category or by name, but stated a problem in search of a solution. And Artery Lock was ready.

This approach worked and each year the business would gain a few new customers, service the existing accounts and hope for the best. There was more business to be had via a more aggressive marketing and sales focus but the owner was satisfied with the return on investment and decided to face each day with a mind toward maintaining the modus operandi that was successful for years.

When the son of the owner took over the business and was looking to make strides in overall business growth and net profits, he decided customer retention was critical and sales and service focus was critical to future success. He looked to install proactive solution selling tactics with a solid product line. The base technical knowledge, inventory and equipment were already in place and they were ready to do more business.

The focus shifted to proactively selling patented key control. Whenever customers called for a re-key or to "change the locks" it was primarily due to one of the following reasons, they had just fired an employee, lost the keys, had keys stolen or had taken over a new property. Artery Lock Dispatch began with the techs asking customers on-site two very important questions to business owners, the first question: "Will you be handing out keys to your employees?" The most popular answer was YES. The second question: "Will it be okay for your employees to have duplicate keys to your business made without your knowledge?" The answer was almost always a resounding NO.

The door was open to provide the right solution. Bear in mind not everyone would opt for the patented key control solution, typically due to financial cost, temporary ownership or managership but when the customer was asked the success rate was over seventy percent!

Owner David Dalessio says, "We learned when we recommend solutions, customers listened over seventy percent of the time. So at Artery Lock we began asking every customer good questions leading to our recommendations. The focused sales of patented key control impacted the business dramatically over a five-year period.

Today over seventy percent of our business is directly related to patented key control systems we have sold. Customers call back again and again. Most often they are adding more doors and buildings to existing systems.

Our customer retention rate is very high due to the sale of proprietary key systems where the customer chooses for Artery Lock to be an exclusive provider, increasing their security by making it virtually impossible for employees to get additional key made without the owner's signature.

There are added bonuses too! Employees have made more money due to the higher dollar sales of patented key control products. Another is that employees leaving my business will not be able to take proprietary keyway system customers with them and that has been a bonus. The business is worth more due to customer documented key systems and customer retention."

When asked about the impact of sales of patented key control in fiscal value to the company was posed, comparing the older version to the transitioned company, David Dalessio said: "There is no question the focus of the past five years has increased annual sales and profits. Our mix of business has changed dramatically. The exchange has been from busy work to more profitable business. We can actually make more doing less. We always want to do more, but rather than just being busy taking every phone call as if it were the only way to survive, we can be more selective and maximize our efforts. The transition has been well worth the pain of change. My brother expounded the virtues of focused selling and patented key control for years, he was right on the money."

As with the first paradigm, the Pro can also be vulnerable to a competitor who has adopted sales oriented business strategies that combine expanded hardware installation capabilities along with greatly improved service offerings and don't wait for the customer to come to them. The competition may have a team of inside sales people as well as professional appearing knowledgeable outside sales people that are out everyday talking to commercial customers, writing and presenting proposals and closing deals. That is a very tough game to beat!

As you might have guessed, these folks represent the next group, which we call the "New Paradigm". This is the business model that has the flexibility and drive needed to succeed as changes in the security hardware business continue to occur and they adjust their product line and expertise accordingly.

The group has positioned itself to do it all. They often market their organization as "Systems Integrators" and have developed a proactive plan that identifies their desirable customer profile and puts resources into play that achieves business relationships that are long term. In many cases, due to extensive customer relations and retention efforts, they avoid even having to participate in a bid process to provide a complete protective barrier plan in place for their customers. Sweet!

We will talk about this business model a lot more in Part II of this book and tell you about how they made the changes to a sales based business and what you can do to make it happen for you!

So who are you? Throughout this book, we will talk about businesses that are in transition as well as those that have completed the paradigm shift from reactive service based to a proactive marketing and sales based organization.

Most of the readers of this book do not fall into any of these models exactly. Instead, elements of all of these models are incorporated into your operations. All of you answer the phone and take orders from callers who find you by letting their fingers do the walking in the yellow book or have been referred to you by others. All of the successful security hardware businesses that we know are led by or employ a variety of technical experts who could probably make a durable lock from scratch in the shop or could go to a commercial customer on a broken camera system DVD call, flip open the case, switch out the mother board and slide in a new hard drive in a few moments and be out the door on their way to the next challenge!

Some people we know in this business while seeming to fall into one or more of the basic operational paradigms, really go beyond the definitions.

It's about high quality personal service

Alarm Company based business owners, like locksmiths often begin with humble origins working as installers for large companies. It usually isn't long before they discover that they are really better off getting their own customers and cutting out the middleman.

A case in point is Rocco D'Erasmo, owner of Continental Alarm, Staten Island, New York. Continental is operated, pretty much by one person, hiring assistants as necessary, working out of a home office and shop.

My own experience with the guy known by most Roy Rogers and Wendy's managers in New York, New Jersey and Philadelphia as just "Rocco, began in 1986. He was working as an installation contractor for a NY City security company I was using and did a great job the first time out. In those days, I was the Regional Loss Prevention Manager in the area working for Marriott Corporation and provided security management for a large group of company owned Roy Rogers Restaurants. Rocco approached me about using him exclusively to install alarms and camera systems and we have worked together for over 20 years.

When I left Marriott to work for Wendy's international, I brought the services of Continental Alarm with me.

Personal service was what differentiated Rocco from the other security providers in the area. Then, as it is now, most of the large companies such as ADT, Honeywell and Wells Fargo Alarm had most of the corporate contracts with national companies. They had lots of sales people selling the jobs but since they often contracted the installations to a variety of small independent companies, they seemed to lack the ability to react to crises when their equipment malfunctioned. Breakdowns and false alarms were the norm due to often-poor installations and the big security companies paid the small companies peanuts to perform service and repairs. Knowing as we do that the money is in the sales, service issues were put on the back burner and response would typically take two to three days to resolve an issue with the alarm or CCTV system.

Continental became the service of choice by always being ahead of the curve with technology. Systems installed by other companies needed service calls to resolve with a technician and could take a number of days during which the system would be down and the business unprotected. Rocco, on the other hand installed panels and software allowing him to dial into a troubled system from his office and pinpoint the problem. Problems that could not be resolved on-line could have a zone bypassed remotely with a follow up service call the next day.

The big deal about this is that Rocco made sure that all of the store managers had his phone numbers. So you, as a closing manager, have a faulty PIR and can't set the alarm system so you can go home? A call to Rocco would result in a work around solution when the panel was tested and the fault found. A store manager that gets to go home on time is a happy guy. And since I never had to get involved in resolving security equipment repairs and lack of service response (like I did with ADT and others), I was happy too! Rocco and I became good friends.

Over time, everyone from the corporate Senior Vice President on down knew whom Rocco was and that he would come through in a crises. He positioned his company to be the on- staff problem solver for all things mechanical and electrical related to our security systems. His camera and alarm systems were so well done, that I don't think he really had that many calls in the middle of the night for service problems. We never ever had false alarm citations for chronically malfunctioning systems like we experienced from other (ADT and others) service providers.

An example of the service level we received occurred in May of 2000. A multiple homicide and robbery occurred at a Wendy's Restaurant in Queens NY. Continental had installed the store alarm and CCTV system.

Key evidence in the case was a missing VCR tape from the time of the murders that was recovered from one of the suspects' homes by NYPD. The tape had been recorded using a multiplexer to convert the analog video to digital and at the time different technologies were not interchangeable and the recovered tape needed to be converted back to standard VHS so detectives could view the tape on other machines and in court if necessary.

Even with all of the technical expertise available to NYPD, detectives reached out to Rocco in the middle of the night who arrived within an hour or two of the call and equipped with the necessary gear converted the tape allowing the detectives to maintain the chain of evidence. I seriously doubt that any of the big named alarm companies could have fielded anything like the service response that Rocco provided that night.

For such a small company, Continental has some pretty impressive big name corporate accounts. Rocco has established his expertise installing IP camera systems for DHL distribution centers among others. One such system involved over 200 cameras to protect a JFK Airport facility.

Rocco told me that his success has been due to keeping up with his technical expertise and taking care of his customers. He said the "technology evolved and I was in the right place and the right time". He also said that "It also helped to keep a low overhead!"

So, even though we describe paradigms as self contained "little boxes", it is really much more complicated for the security product hardware business owner to analyze their position in the marketplace and what direction should be taken to maximize the odds of success.

We need sales like this!

Daryl figures out that his business is way too reactive!

An exercise you can use to identify your model is called a "SWOT" analysis. This model is very basic but can ask some very important questions that you need to have answered before you can identify all of the elements of a successful business plan. It can be especially effective when operations management and your key employees get involved in the process. You will find that the results can give you a lot more information that you need to make planning changes that your organization may need to move forward in order to be more competitive and profitable. It's called working together or "Synergy" a combined effect greater than their separate effects.

We suggest that you take out a piece of paper and pencil and answer the following questions. Put the completed page in the back of the book so that we can review some of your answers later. Write this down, it's important!

SWOT = Strengths – Weaknesses – Opportunities - Threats

The "S" represents the question where you make a list of your "Strengths". What do you do really well? Can you deliver, for instance, a level of service way beyond your customers' expectations? Way better than your competitors? Do you provide many more types of services than your competitors can? List them all now.

List your technical skills and those within your organization. What are you really good at? Have you leveraged your skills to position your business ahead of the competition?

When you are done with this first section, most of you will have a pretty extensive list of all of the things that you know how to do really well. The list represents your competitive advantage in the marketplace. The question is "Do your customers know that you can do all of this stuff?" The answer will shape what you need to focus on in your marketing and advertising plan.

Perhaps it's time to invite all of your customers to a customer appreciation event that includes expert speakers conversation and problem solving. Or how about a small business security clinic?

The "W" is the question of what your competitive weaknesses are. We have every hope that this will be the shortest list in your analysis, but you really need to be brutally honest with yourself when writing down what your weaknesses are.

This list will certainly include any barriers that exist that prevent you from being competitive. Perhaps it is an issue of financing or lack of necessary credentials, licenses or knowledge. What are you not doing that is allowing your competitors to take business away from you?

The answers to your negative attributes will prompt you to ask important questions. Is it time to analyze how your capital is allocated? Should you be spending less on yellow book ads and develop more proactive sales strategies? Should you be looking at what needs to happen to grow your businesses skills to be able to respond to technological changes? Should your next hire be a specialist in skills that your organization does not currently have? Do you need to personally acquire more personal management skills or technical skills?

The "O" asks you to identify what unrealized Opportunities exist on your radar. Even the most mature organization in terms of longevity and experience can develop a blind side and miss obvious opportunities. The missed opportunity can actually be telegraphed to our customers with some undesired results,

For instance, we know several alarm based companies that state in their ads and even their websites that they do not deal with mechanical locks. Have they blown off a potential customer who now will not call because he thinks he needs his locks fixed and you have told him that there is nothing that you can do for him? Having missed the call, have you lost the opportunity to recommend getting rid of his old insecure mechanical locks and selling him on the benefits of a stand alone electronic lock system or even an integrated PC based one? By refusing to take the time to have the conversation, you miss the opportunity to ask the right questions that can bring in more business.

We have noticed many locksmith-based businesses that simply do not want to deal with electronic security components. Whether it is a skill based issue or just is outside of the normal work comfort zone, saying "no" to customer requests cannot bode well for the future of the enterprise.

The opportunity list, hopefully, will be as long and varied as your strengths list and should urge the question of "If we're not going after a significant piece of the business, why not?" Missed opportunities beg for a complete analysis of whether current resources can be used to go after the prize. Has the enterprise developed the flexibility to change when they need to on their own initiative or are they forced to try new processes and technology as a survival mechanism?

The "T" asks the question to identify all of the Threats that can make the enterprise fail at worst and merely show modestly declined revenue and profits at best. The list of what can go wrong can be endless and tedious but must be recognized so that a countering strategy can be put in place. It is rather like investing in the financial market. A good balance of stocks and bonds can protect your assets from large swings in the marketplace.

You should always start an organizational threat list with the worst-case scenarios. Start with catastrophic loss due to a fire or weather event like a flood. Don't forget to add all of the next tier of possible losses due to potential exposure to traffic accidents involving one of your trucks, a serious workers compensation or customer liability claim, a crime loss to your business, liability exposure resulting in your being sued for either something that you did, or worse, failed to do.

By the way, did you know that 30% of all business bankruptcies are a result of employee theft or embezzlement? This list should give the business owner pause to consider whether potential losses are either insured against or exposure reduced through sound company policies, procedures and work rules that you have initiated to protect your investment. You have done that, right?

So you have completed the four lists and surrounded by your managers and trusted key employees you can now ask the necessary questions about what you need to do to create an environment where change isn't quite as frightening and progress to a specific list of potential actions and list multiple activities that address what needs to be done, who will do it and when the activity will be completed.

We suggest that you take out another piece of paper and pencil and answer the following questions. Put the completed page in the back of the book so that you can review some of your answers later.

What is your paradigm?
Sales driven or production driven?
Aggressively promote your customer retention program?

Wait for the phone to ring?

What barriers have you established requiring you to turn down a job?

How does your customer see you?
- As a business professional operating from a retail business at one or more locations,   wears business attire?
- A phone number in the book, works from a truck, wears Dickies with a nametag?

How do you see yourself?
Pro?
Worker bee?
Tradesman or Businessman?

What is the sales growth current trend in your business?
Trend is "Up"-can't keep up with it?
Very busy but keeping less profit margin?
Flat versus last year?

What is your long-term apparent sales trend?
- Steady upward growth?
- Working hard to just stay even?
- Trending downward as competition and operating costs increases?

What is your flow through profit trend?
- Expansion?
- Even?
- Net lower?

What you do best?
Lock pro?
Electrical?
Safecracker?
Doors?

What are your competitors better at?
Systems?
Create one system out of multiple components?
Why can't you do that?

Do you have a plan to learn new disciplines?
Classes?
Trade shows?

Seminars?

If industry trends show a new direction, can you adapt?
Recognize?
Plan?
Change?

Do you have written business plans?
New each year?
Goals are measurable?
Activities focus on achieving goals?
Budget line items for all cost centers?

Do you have a Business Exit Plan, Succession Plan or Business Continuity
Planning Strategies?
- Sell it?
- Liquidate?
- Leave it to _____.

Who Are You?

Who Do You Want To
Be?

How Do You Make It
Happen?

Meanwhile over on 2nd Ave....

Chapter 2

Marketing 101

Daryl looks for the smart
ways of doing business!

Chapter 2   Marketing 101

This chapter contains a lot of "meat and potatoes" to open up the subject of exactly what marketing is and how it can impact your business bottom line in a predictable way. Since the purpose of this book is to get you thinking about creating a new plan to market your security hardware based business, we wanted to start our dialog with some basic information and commentary about the topic of marketing and work on defining some of the terms that we will be using in this book.

For instance, when we talk about "Vertical Markets" we really mean your existing customer base. This group of customers that you regularly take care of represents the core value of your business. It is the basis of potential sales that is most likely to provide you with recurring income cash flow as well as larger more complex jobs that are gained as a result of building relationships of trust and often without having to bid competitively. You can call it "old business".

We cannot overstate the value of taking care of your existing customers. Most marketing professionals state that it costs your business 5 times as much to get one new customer versus taking care of and keeping your existing ones. Think about it when you sit down to do your annual business plan and determine what you will spend on advertising and what you anticipate the results will be. Will it bring in business that may take the place of the existing customers and potential revenue that you already have because you will not be able to take the time needed to keep it? If so, what's the point unless you are willing to expand your staff and equipment to take on the new business? There are lots of competitors out there ready to take away your existing customers if you fail to maintain relationships.

New business, of course, refers to all of the store floor traffic and the response calls that involve sales and jobs for customers that you haven't dealt with before. New business also includes your inside and outside sales calls to people that you want to do business with. Everything that is not old business is new business!

New business is finite within your geographical area. That means there are a set number of potential new customers inside of the geographical area that it is profitable for you to work in. You can also call it your "trade area" and it is certainly possible in the absence of a large new population influx to reach a saturation point where between you and your competitors, just about all of your products are being sold that are going to be sold. In other words, everybody who wants what you have to sell already has one! They simply won't buy anymore until the one they now have breaks, becomes obsolete or something brand new comes along that they like better and must have.

In order for you to gain additional pools of potential new customers, you have to develop a presence in the new trade area. By the way, other competitors may already saturate new trade areas!

Where are your new customers coming from?

Advertising may be bringing in a regular flow of new sales and some of the work is profitable and some jobs are less profitable due to higher labor and material costs not all of which can be passed to the consumer due to issues of market competition. Ads placed in newspapers, trade journals and the yellow pages are all common forms of advertising. They are also expensive and require annual renewal to maintain your presence. It is also difficult to quantify exactly which publication is actually bringing in the business resulting in an inefficient effort.

Some other great advertising we see is creative artwork on service trucks and the transformation of real estate such as your shop building into a visual and recognizable landmark. That means when someone drives by and sees your storefront, they immediately flash on an image of what you do.

Referral business is among the best sort of new business since the person coming to your shop or is calling is doing so based on another customers satisfied experience. That means your "old business" is creating a flow of "new business" at no extra cost to you!

Is your marketing production driven marketing – getting the customer to come to you? Many of these techniques are very effective in driving work and keep many security company businesses very busy.

JoeyD's Lessons From Successes.

Another transition….this one over one hundred years!

Bellingham Lock & Safe began in 1904 when Hugh Diehl and Charlie Stanbra started a bicycle and locksmith business. Not long after that, Hugh left the business to pursue Indian brand motorcycles and eventually the Ford dealership. Pollard retained control of the business for many years but eventually sold the locksmith portion of the business to a gentleman named Bus Charles.

Bus ran the locksmith operation in a building in the 1300 block of Railroad Avenue until his death in the early 1950's. Four months later, Gus Newman moved to Bellingham to pick up the mantle. He was sole proprietor until present day owner Jim Vos joined him as partner in 1971. When Gus felt it was time to retire and move to Hawaii, his son-in-law Link Shadley took over his half of the business. Link and Jim expanded the business in the early '80's until Jim took complete responsibility for Bellingham Lock & Safe when Link left to pursue other work. Because of the continuing growth, Jim moved the business to its current location on North State Street. The 10,000 square foot facility today houses a family of over 30 employees.

The company diversified in one unusual way by acquiring a local company that sold and serviced fire extinguishers. The fire suppression business provides a very nice twist in that all public buildings must be inspected on a routine basis. While inspecting and servicing vital safety equipment, a look about to make sure security and codes were met really opened the door to new business.

Jim Vos once said while our traditional lock and safe business is steady and we have a lot of clients, not too many leads for fire extinguishers sales and service pops out, however quite the opposite is true, it has been a great marriage.

The company now has a full complement of security and safety products and services including fire suppression, contract hardware, surveillance systems, access controls and alarm systems. Because of this growth, the new name Security Solutions was introduced around the turn of the New Century, (2000) to more accurately reflect this complete offering.

Bellingham Lock & Safe will continue to provide superior lock and safe products and services, and through Security Solutions, address all security needs in Northwest Washington.

Over the last 25 years the electronic security portion of Bellingham Lock & Safe has gown to be the largest division of the company further supporting the introduction of the new name Security Solutions. This division handles a wide range of security needs including; burglar alarms, fire alarms, intercom systems, access control systems, biometric access products, CCTV surveillance systems, and more.

The key to success in addition to vision and financial wherewithal is the people and the level of commitment to do things right and completely. The technicians have a combined experience of nearly 100 years. The company offers everything from project design to installation, to programming, and service. Jamie Vos, GM says "What has set us apart from other competitors over the last 25 years has been service, service, service. We pride ourselves in our service department, which in this industry is a must. A non working security system is not security at all."

You can see the recurring theme. Lock and keys are not the sole components of security anymore.

The term "Sales Driven Marketing" , defined as finding and selling to the desired customer profile is another way of selling new business. Geography is a factor as is demographics and customer profiling. The idea is to identify the profile of the customer and products they typically use and to aggressively use sales people to contact and sell your products and services. The goal is to seek out high profit jobs and control labor and over-head costs such as holding a lot of excess little used inventory. Proactive sales driven marketing positions the business to be less dependant on advertising and having to take the less profitable jobs that come in as the "pot luck" flow of service requests are handled. Inventory is held on frequently used products only with most inventory arriving from the parts wholesalers on a planned delivery schedule to meet the job production requirements. Remember, inventory is money. If it's not flying off the shelf, it's not contributing to the growth of your cash flow.

Sales driven proactive organizations have less need to invest in the tools and technicians needed to respond to emergency calls resulting in reduced overtime labor and service cost. It's sort of like better planning equates to less chaos. Less chaos equals less stress on you and your people.

The term viral marketing was originally penned in a newsletter by venture capitalist Steve Jurvetson, who defined it as "network-enhanced word of mouth." While the word "viral" may have negative connotations ("the flu" and "corrupted hard drive" come to mind), the concept of viral marketing is a positive one.

Marketers have long believed that people who hear about a product or service from a friend are more likely to buy, and buy more quickly and easily than those who heard about it in other ways. In fact, many articles on viral marketing make reference to a classic 1970's Clairol TV commercial with a sudsy-headed women who told two friends, and then "they told two friends, and so on and so on and so on." While that commercial is probably the easiest way to illustrate the concept of viral marketing, it's not the most helpful example because: (1) most of us can't afford to produce a TV commercial, and (2) now, with the Internet, and E-mail in particular, you can tell more people about something faster than good-old-fashioned word of mouth.

Ask yourself some of the following to begin the process of being able to identify your primary and secondary strategies that you use to grow your business. The answers can tell you about your business plan process.

What are the marketing costs you incur annually?
Marketing Staff?
Ads of all sorts?
Trinkets and logo items?
Other costs? (List)

Do you budget your anticipated marketing costs as a percentage of sales?
What percent?
Criteria or specific marketing methods that you budget. (list)
Goals that you want to achieve with each expenditure type. (list)

What percent of marketing dollars are devoted to new business acquisition?
Percent of total sales?
Goals of the expenditure?
Measures you use to show success

What percent of marketing dollars are left for existing customers?
Percent of total?
Goals you list?
Effectiveness of your program?

Is your customer base commercial versus residential?
List reasons why you choose this target market
Profitability?
Growth?

Who is your primary target customer?
Main St. B-to-B?
New construction?
Retrofit?
Emergency service?
Automotive?
Residential?

Which type customers are the most profitable for you?

Which type customers are less profitable?

Are there reasons for taking better care of existing customers?

Do you plan existing customer retention strategies?

How do you measure the effectiveness of your marketing plan?

Have you created recurring income strategies?

Have you established full Preventative Maintenance recurring fee or re-duced/discounted rate membership with a recurring fee?

What strategies do you have in place for accessing and educating your customers?

What strategies do you use to explain all of your available service offerings?

Answer all of these questions and you have some of the raw materials need-ed for a written marketing plan!

**What's your customer and product mix?
Are you focusing your energy on the
Most profitable segments?**

Chapter 3

Finding Out
What Your
Customer
Really Needs

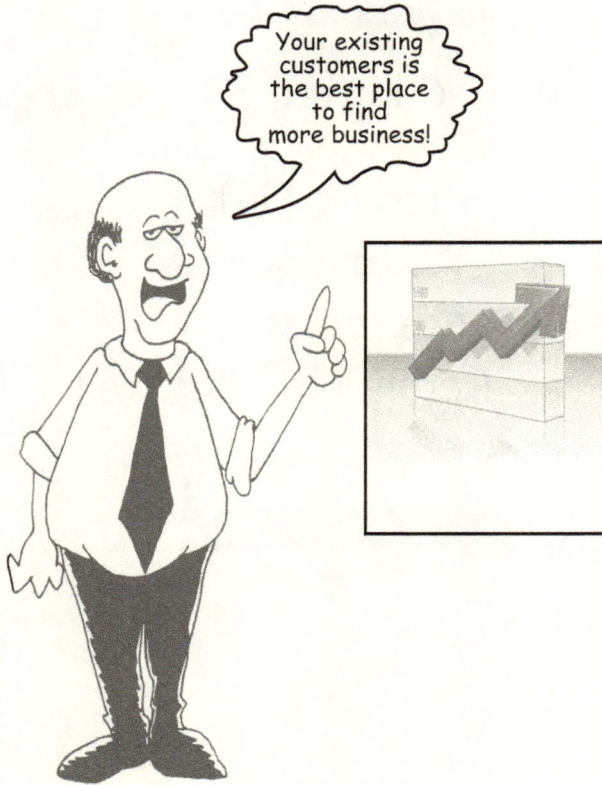

Daryl knows that he needs to find out
more about what his customers need!

Chapter 3   Finding Out What Your Customer Really Needs

Why should you perform surveys for all sites where work is performed? Whether you find yourself at a commercial address or a customers home or car, you will always need to conduct at least a brief checklist that establishes the scope of the current job. Most importantly, however, a survey will help you to develop an organized approach to every job and serves as a basis to propose additional projects that bring you more revenue. More revenue is good!

The on-site survey is one of the first steps that you need to take to transition from being reactive to proactive. The depth of the survey can go from very basic to very complex depending on your perception of the return on investment for your time.

What that means is, for example, that a service job to repair a CCTV system or get someone into something that they are locked out of will began with the basic customer information that you complete and can progress to a comprehensive loss prevention system survey you will need to complete for a commercial customer as a basis for an integrated systems proposal.

The first part of the information that you gather identifies and details who your customer is and forms a basis for the data you need about your new customer for your E-mail advertising program and the in-depth information that forms the basis for equipment and other program recommendations that will make sense to your customer. You need more information beyond what the customer tells you that he wants you to do in order to be able to explain what is the correct way to solve the stated problem or loss exposure. What they want and what should be done are often two different things, as any service pro will tell you!

What if your customer wants something that is not compatible with existing systems or worse, non- compliant due to regulatory issues or published standards?

We had an example a number of years ago with an employer who acquired a group of restaurants from a franchisee. Some 20 sites had been developed and every site had non-compliant door hardware installed by the same locksmith company. It was what the franchise owner told the lock company they wanted – double keyed deadbolts on the doors.

Since doors in a commercial establishment must be able to allow emergency exit to occur with no more than one motion, only allowing exit to the possessor of a key once the store closes to the public, is a violation of every states fire code that we are aware of. One motion would include pushing a panic bar to release the latch. Refusing to install illegal hardware is the duty of care of every ethical security hardware service company.

We still hear from companies that install CCTV systems that they still occasionally receive customer requests to install "dummy" or inoperative cameras for "show". You really do need to explain to some people that they invite lawsuits when they consider installing fake systems on the cheap to address the need for a real preventative tool such as a surveillance camera!

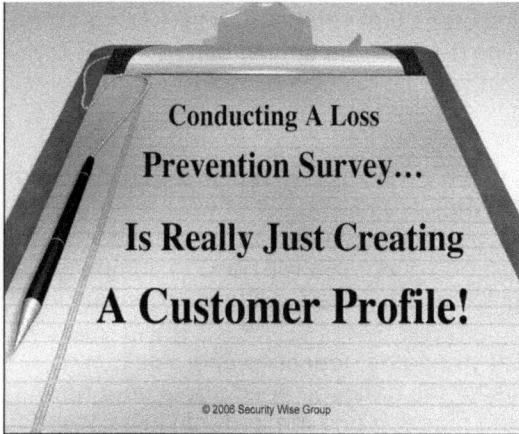

Conducting A Loss Prevention Survey... Is Really Just Creating A Customer Profile!

© 2006 Security Wise Group

What survey tools should you use? There are a number of types that you can use. Some emphasize the purely mechanical systems questions, and others include customer operational questions as well in order to determine what systems are likely to be the most beneficial and will be correctly managed by the end user customer.

All persons providing security services or equipment need to be aware of the fact that there are published professional standards that govern what constitutes a security survey and what results recommended equipment must perform to meet the standards.

Did you know that an agency of the federal government has issued a guideline that sets a performance standard regarding how a camera system should be installed in a commercial business? That performance standards state where the cameras should go? What the quality of the image should be for playback? That the standard specifically references banks and convenience stores? That the agency in question is none other than the Forensic Science Division of the FBI? The Department Of Homeland Security!

If your company is in the business of selling and installing camera systems, you may want to take a few minutes to peruse this article and obtain a copy of the standards at the Forensic Division website http://www.fbi.gov/hq/lab/fsc/backissu/jan2005/index.htm

The standard is published in two parts and in Part 1 addresses system design, recording systems, cameras, media, system maintenance, retention

of recordings and evidence handling. The stated purpose of these requirements is to "increase the likelihood that images recovered from CCTV systems are sufficient to enable law enforcement officials to identify people and
objects depicted therein".

Part 2 of the standard deals very specifically with the use and installation
of cameras in banks and convenience store applications. Floor plans are
included. This soup to nuts approach appears to be intended as a standard
for all retail applications. As you can imagine, the government would like to
see the days of crappy unviewable video from crime scenes to be a thing of
the past. The only way they see that dream becoming an eventual reality after viewing miles and miles of fuzzy bank robbery video, is to publish a clear
document of standards stating how the system is supposed to work.

So why is this important to you as the recommender and installer of security
equipment? Is it because of your potential liability exposure in the event
that your customer is sued following a crime loss or an event involving injury
to one of their customers? Would you have some responsibility if the person
suing your customer proves in court that the equipment that you recommended and installed failed to meet published standards and to perform its
stated purpose resulting in injury to their client?

We don't know for sure because we are not lawyers. We are, however,
experienced at getting sued for alleged inadequate security resulting in a
claimed monetary loss/injury/death to a customer or invitee or employee on
the premises of a former corporate employer. For the most part the suits
were settled for fairly insignificant amounts or were dismissed. That was,
however, before a number of published security standards began to emerge
after 2001.

As a Regional Loss Prevention Manager for the Big Company (read deep
pockets) getting sued, guess who had to go to the deposition and defend
what security systems, policies and procedures were used and why? For
the most part, since there were no published standards, only general industry practices for comparison, it was fairly simple to show that not only did the
company provide reasonable care for the customer/plaintiffs safety but actually exceeded the level of protective systems that were provided in similar
establishments in areas with similar crime history. Therefore our attorneys
would argue, while extraordinary barriers could have been possibly able to
prevent the event from occurring, the likelihood of such an injury event occurring was simply not foreseeable. Case dismissed!

Published standards, on the other hand, can give a plaintiffs' attorney a potential blue print to follow to determine if a case might exist that could allow

some money damages to be extracted from a company obliged to provide reasonable care of his client, "the victim".

The standards that get published can come from a number of directions that you need to know about. As mentioned above, the folks at Homeland Security are now in the business of publishing standards that may or may not be widely known even to the industry segment expected to follow them. The CCTV standard has been around since July 2004. It came to our attention when a lecture was attended in Maryland a while back and an FBI Forensic Division agent explained the program with a PowerPoint presentation to a room full of law enforcement and loss prevention managers.

Other standards on other topics are also being written by industry professional organizations such as ASIS International. ASIS is a 50-year-old professional security management organization that established the Certified Protection Professional program. In the last few years since ASIS was designated as a primary standards creator by the American National Standards Institute (ANSI) they have published standards related to security survey methodology, chief security officer standards and security guard training standards. It is clear that other standards are in the pipeline and will include their own versions of security equipment implementation in commercial environments.

What all of this means to all of us in the loss prevention industry, especially if your role includes recommending and installing security hardware, is you must be aware that in the future published standards will require us to stay on top of current technology. It becomes imperative that the hardware we sell meets the performance standards that are published.

It becomes a duty of your profession to make your customers aware of the security system performance standards that affect their industry in order to adequately protect their business from potential liability exposure. Locksmithing, Electronic Security and Alarm Systems may be your trade, but your profession is Loss Prevention Systems Integration. To the majority of commercial customers that you provide solutions, products, installation and service to every day, you are the only security professional that they know! And it is what you know that can help their business reduce loss exposure and improve revenue to your company.

The creation of all of these standards also makes the role of a properly designed loss prevention survey a must have program to offer your customers. Without an in-depth investigation of your customers existing systems, policies and procedures, a realistic recommendation for improvement to your customers' ability to protect their people and assets may not be accurate or adequate. By offering this free service to your customers, you also increase your value to their goal of maintaining a profitable return on their investment.

Many times, even a modest investment on equipment and written policies and procedures, can recover a percentage of the customer's losses quickly enough to be very noticeable. To make the process work, you need to get a good estimate of what your customer is losing and writing off due to the lack of prevention programs.

Factors such as geographical location, demographics and the value of assets that need protection will vary the need for protective strategies. However, some minimum basics must be in place in all business enterprises that include locks on the doors, a safe place to keep valuables and cash, policies to manage the people and procedures to control and account for money and inventory flow. In some businesses it's simple and it is complex in others.

Being able to use the survey method as an information-gathering tool appears to work with less resistance if presented as a benefit to your customer that does not require them to get out their checkbook. Think about it. When was the last time that you completed somebody's survey that wanted to charge you for it? How about if you perceived that the answers that you provide to a survey, will produce a personalized report or improvement recommendations that would help you run your business better?

The survey process is a time investment you make in order to collect the information about your customers you need in order to provide a higher level of service. By gaining a greater understanding of your customers needs, you open the door to more sales opportunities.

The survey we use at Security Wise Group LLC®, was designed to simply determine what basic procedures, company policies and security systems are missing from the end user company. The survey is very general in nature because every business has different Strengths, Weaknesses, Opportunities and Threats that creates their unique loss exposure profile.

In the next section we will deal with the survey content and what our responses would be anticipated typically depending on how each question is answered. Remember that the survey is general in nature and simply cannot address all of the issues that may need to be addressed in a particular business. We always make sure that we note questions that arise as a result of the survey when answers don't fall into the "Yes or No" columns.

The Survey form illustrated on the next 2 pages is a simplified version of the ASIS survey tool that is available on line at their website asisonline.com.

SWG
Security Wise Group
"Your Loss Prevention Department"

Loss Prevention Survey© (Rev. 11/2005)

Organization Information:

Name of Company:		Primary Address:		
Type of Enterprise:		Number of Locations:	Date of Application:	
Application Sponsor:		Sponsor Number:	Completed by:	

Name, Title, Address and Phone # for primary and secondary contacts:

Name:	Title:	Phone:		Cell:
Address:	City:	State:	Zip:	E-Mail:
Name:	Title:	Phone:		Cell:
Address:	City:	State:	Zip:	E-Mail:

In order to serve you better, we need to know more about your existing systems.

* Your Average Unit Volume = $_____ per year.

Retail store percentage of gross sales you estimate to be "shrink" or loss. For restaurants food cost variance between actual usage (beginning vs. ending inventory) and theoretical (what you sold).

1% ☐   2% ☐   3% ☐   4% ☐   Over 5% ☐

I.   Physical Security

1. Describe exterior door access locks for all locations. (electronic access control? Keyed deadbolt? Crashbar inside, cylinder outside etc.)

_____

2. Does the ingress/egress hardware meet local and state fire code?   Yes ☐   No ☐
3. List all exterior door lock system corrections.   None   ☐

_____

4. List any missing/malfunctioning interior door locks, closers, crashbars etc.

_____

5. Written polices are in place to enforce key control and access rules. Yes ☐   No ☐
6. A burglary rated safe is in each location that handles money or valuables. Yes ☐   No ☐
7. All safes are electronic time lock that are programmed to allow individual combinations. Yes ☐   No ☐
8. Is there a burglar alarm in each location?   Yes ☐   No ☐
9. Does the system adaquately protect the building interior after close?   Yes ☐   No ☐
10. List the name of the alarm monitoring company for all locations.

II.   Cash Controls

11. The business has an electronic POS system to record sales activity. Yes ☐ No ☐
12. The business has written cash control policies.   Yes ☐ No ☐

13. Managers and employees are trained and acknowledged written policies.   Yes ☐ No ☐
14. Register sales activity flows to a back of the house manager's workstation?   Yes ☐ No ☐
15. All operators have their own cash drawer.   Yes ☐ No ☐
16. Each location has a CCTV system.   Yes ☐   No ☐
17. Cameras and recording is digital (DVR).   Yes ☐   No ☐
18. List what locations are viewed. (i.e. Registers, back door, office, sales area, outside lots etc.)

_____

19. List locations not covered that should be.

_____

20. Written procedures are in place related to the use of CCTV equipment and operation
    of the DVR/Recorder.   Yes ☐   No ☐
21. This business has written security procedures. (i.e. Theft, burglary, robbery prevention and
    response, disturbances, trespass, etc.)   Yes ☐   No ☐
22. Does this company employ security personnel?   Yes ☐   No ☐
23. If Yes, are they in-house or contract. If contract, name of company providing service.

_____

III.   Human Resource issues

24. Does this business have a person assigned to HR/Benefits?   Yes ☐   No ☐
25. If Yes, are HR issues handled in-house or with a contract company. List contract company.

_____

26. The business has issued an employee handbook.   Yes ☐   No ☐
27. Is there a written disciplinary action policy?   Yes ☐   No ☐
28. The company conducts new hire orientation where all company policies, procedures and
    rules are explained.   Yes ☐   No ☐
29. Employees and managers receive a copy of the rules and sign an acknowledgement form.
    Yes ☐   No ☐
30. A back ground investigation is conducted on all new employees.   Yes ☐   No ☐
31. A background investigation is conducted for managers/supervisors.   Yes ☐   No ☐
32. Workers Compensation and customer claims are centrally reported to an assigned person
    and logged.   Yes ☐   No ☐
33. The business has a written safety policy/program in place.   Yes ☐   No ☐
34. Safety hazards are identified and corrected using an inspection report process.   Yes ☐   No ☐

This survey is general in nature since no survey can address all of the vulnerabilities of various types of business enterprises. However, many businesses experience losses due to common reasons. The purpose of this survey is to identify possible control weaknesses that may be decreasing profits. Security Wise Group®, will provide a written response outlining the control issues we find, along with programs available that can help you recover some of your profits. The survey is for planning purposes only, and no other warranties or guarantees are made or implied that you will recover losses and no survey can address all of the loss prevention issues facing your business.

As part of our continuing service to our SWG® member companies, an in-depth system audit is available on a fee per service plus expense basis.

Signature of Business Representative: _____ **Date:** _____

Signature of Security Specialist: _____ **Date:** _____

We find that it is the in-between issues that may open up a totally different strategy to protect a particular business environment. It pays to find out from your customer what problems they are experiencing so don't be afraid to ask the questions.

For example, not long ago I spoke with a dealer who was called by a customer who owned a number of "Jiffy" type oil change locations. He was being plagued by customer claims regarding body damage allegedly occurring during the service process. Following the installation of a camera system in the service bays, claims decreased to zero. Anytime a customer complained, the manager and customer could view the condition of the car as it entered the bay, what occurred during servicing and what it looked like when the customer reclaimed it.

The customer also learned that the camera system could reduce his exposure to register theft and phony Workers Compensation claims.

The following pages preview the survey and explain the rationale behind the questions that we ask. Remember this is just one approach and your job, when you are conducting a survey, is to anticipate and identify additional questions or details that will be needed in order for the proposal to be generated.

Name of Company:			Primary Address:		
Type of Enterprise:			Number of Locations:		Date of Survey:
Sponsor:			Sponsor Number:		Completed by:
Name, Title, Address and Phone # for primary and secondary contacts:					
Name:	Title:		Phone:		Cell:
Address:	City:		State:	Zip:	E-Mail:
Name:	Title:		Phone:		Cell:
Address:	City:		State:	Zip:	E-Mail:

The first section of our survey gathers important information about the customer and identifies the "Primary Decision Maker" within the customer's organization. All loss prevention programs must have "top down" support to succeed, so you need to establish a relationship with the top of the "food chain". At a minimum, your primary contact must be the person with direct responsibility for establishing and enforcing policies and procedures and controls the budget for any capital improvements necessary.

A section identifying the Loss Prevention partner company conducting the survey is provided and must be completed for our records.

The next survey section we use seeks to identify financial information necessary for the process to proceed.

It should be noted that many business owners will not discuss their specific sales information with you. However, you need to establish what the sales and shrinkage amounts are in order to build the justification argument to expand or improve your customers loss prevention program.

In order to serve you better, we need to know more about your existing systems.
* Your Average Unit Volume = $_____ per year.

Retail store percentage of gross sales you estimate to be "shrink" or loss. For restaurants food cost variance between actual usage (beginning vs. ending inventory) and theoretical (what you sold).
    1%   2%   3%   4%   Over 5%

In our experience, the answer is to identify the industry averages and ask your customer if their sales and losses are within the average. For example available information on-line at websites identifies the average 7-11 convenience store sales as averaging $1,714,000 in annual sales. All you have to do to obtain information from a public company is to obtain total sales from website financials and divide by the number of operational units. Non public companies will have similar sales.

Many industry trade groups will publish shrinkage survey results as reported by their members. For instance, the Food Marketing Institute reports that their members lose 2.32% of sales to shrinkage. Big box retailers publish shrink percentage at 1.6% of sales after spending another .5% for loss prevention people and programs. This number may be on the "light" side, as losses for small to midsize retail companies tend to be greater due to lack of controls by two or three times the average.

The key is to do some research and consult prior to conducting the survey. The information found on-line is huge and a little research makes you the smartest person in the room when discussing potential losses with your customers.

Survey questions 1 - 4 asks you to determine if the business access controls are adequate to keep out unauthorized persons during periods when the business is closed and controls the access to cash and stock areas when the business is open. This section is a major opportunity for the security hardware professional conducting the survey to create a teaching moment with the owner and inform them regarding state of the art key control and electronic access control systems that are available and are becoming increasingly affordable to all businesses regardless of size.

This is a place that you will need to take detailed notes regarding the current store lock systems and determine whether the systems that are being observed are the same in all of the business locations. Take pictures or draw a diagram of all access control points.

It is amazing how some companies expand and do not integrate access controls with their existing locations but simply accept whatever hardware is included in the new location. Integration is a major sales opportunity for new hardware and future preventative maintenance program proposals.

I. Physical Security

1. Describe exterior door access locks for all locations. (Electronic access control? Keyed dead bolt? Crashbar inside, cylinder outside etc.)

2. Does the ingress/egress hardware meet local and state fire code?   Yes   No
3. List all exterior door lock system corrections.   None

4. List any missing/malfunctioning interior door locks, closers, crashbars etc.

Written policies are needed to set the rules and expectations needed to maintain the integrity of the access control or even a mechanical lock system. No sense in locking the doors, if you don't know where all of your keys are. Worse, they may be in the possession of a dishonest ex-employee!

---

5. Written polices are in place to enforce key control and access rules. Yes   No

---

Questions 6 & 7 pertain to money safes. A "rated safe" means a UL rated safe that is burglary rated and not just fire rated. Electronic access safes have paid for themselves many times over, in our experience, by allowing the programming of individual combinations, unauthorized lock-out windows and an audit feature that allows the owner/operator of the business to identify who entered the safe and when.

If they are not equipped with the right safe to control cash, there is an obvious opportunity now or in the future to recommend the right solution.

> 6. A burglary rated safe is in each location that handles money or valuables.   Yes   No
> 7. All safes are electronic time lock that are programmed to allow individual combinations.   Yes   No

Questions 8 - 10 ask about burglary protection, a basic need in all businesses.   Unfortunately, in our experience, many of these systems are improperly
installed and maintained creating virtual havoc in the form of false alarms
and monitoring company calls to the business owner at 3:00 AM.   False
alarms are a huge expense to public law enforcement and many police departments will eventually not respond to alarm calls if you have many false
alarms.   In fact, the owner usually starts receiving citations and fines if the
problem is not corrected.

> 8. Is there a burglar alarm in each location?   Yes   No
> 9. Does the system adequately protect the building interior after close?   Yes   No
> 10. List the name of the alarm monitoring company for all locations.

The Security Hardware Professional should determine if the system is
functional and protects the areas of the buildings where cash and valuables
are kept.   Our rule of thumb is that protection should start at the money safe
and radiate outward from that point and include detection sensors covering
pathways leading to the safe.

Doors should be contacted and large open areas covered by PIR sensors.
A strobe light and siren should be located near the front of the building.

Each business has different protection requirements and some alarm service providers are proficient and some are not.   We recommend that you
obtain the name of the current provider along with information about when
any existing contracts expire.

Upgrading and replacing the company alarm system is another major sales
opportunity.

There is no question that if your business handles cash, a point of sale
cash register system is a must.   The equipment can be virtually worthless,
however, if written policies and procedures are not in place governing how
cash is to be handled.   The implementation of rules is necessary in order to
set expectations and to create an audit trail so that individuals can be held
accountable in the event of a shortage or loss.

II. Cash Controls
11. The business has an electronic POS system to record sales activity.   Yes   No
12. The business has written cash control policies.   Yes   No
13. Managers and employees are trained and acknowledged written policies.   Yes   No
14. Register sales activity flows to a back of the house manager's workstation.   Yes   No
15. All operators have their own cash drawer.   Yes   No

This question is of great importance to loss prevention people like us, security hardware installers need to be aware of what the correct practices should be in place to control cash in any retail business because if the internal controls are lacking, loss opportunities increase. Even if you are not prepared to offer advice you may be able to recommend a professional that can help.

CCTV systems are another basic business commodity needed to protect store assets and can be a deterrent to theft, robbery and false accident claims. It needs to be stated that there can be a lot of poor quality or out-dated camera systems hanging on your customer's walls. If poor equipment is used, improperly installed or not maintained, the systems are another waste of money.

16. Each location has a CCTV system.   Yes   No
17. Cameras and recording is digital (DVR).   Yes   No
18. List what locations are viewed. (i.e. Registers, back door, office, sales area, outside lots etc.)
_____
19. List locations not covered that should be.
_____
20. Written procedures are in place related to the use of CCTV equipment and operation
     of the DVR/Recorder.   Yes   No

The good news is that there are many very good affordable digital camera systems available that will make your end user customer very happy the first time they are able to use the system to catch a thief or thwart a false slip and fall claim. The key opportunity here is to convince your customer to take the plunge and make use of this tool to better manage the business.

The purpose of the next 3 questions is to determine if the business has written security procedures governing employee actions in the event of theft, burglary, robbery, altercations, trespassers etc.

21. This business has written security procedures. (i.e. theft, burglary, robbery prevention and
     response, disturbances, trespass, etc.)   Yes   No
22. Does this company employ security personnel?   Yes   No
23. If Yes, are they in-house or contract. If contract, name of company providing service.
_____

Without these policies in place, the business is exposed to civil liability if reasonable care is not performed to protect customers and employees. Our company security expert has a number of written programs available to help your customers establish a security procedures and response plan. Your knowledge about where to go to get help with these policy issues is a plus for your customer relationship.

Identified use of security personnel, such as guards, in any of the business' locations, should be responded to with a careful review before making your recommendations to your customer. Guards are expensive, often inefficient and can cause more problems then they solve if not managed properly.

Many companies that use guards, without on site in-house professional supervision, experience less than stellar performance from guard companies due to a number of factors including poor selection and training, bad super-vision and high turnover. And there are often many cost effective alterna-tives to using guards such as remotely monitored interactive video systems that have personnel respond verbally online and view any reported distur-bance when an alarm button is pressed. Recommending a cost effective proposal that includes replacing high cost-low results programs is your job and will forward your goal of maintaining good customer relations.

The HR Section is another place where we need you to look at some is-sues that you may not have addressed before with customers. This section relates to specific issues that will make or break security hardware and loss prevention programs.

Most of the losses occurring in your customers business are due to em-ployee's actions or omissions. If your customer is not paying attention to HR basics and employees are not accountable due to lack of policies and procedures, losses will surely occur. By the way, that goes for any business enterprise including your own!

III. Human Resource issues

24. Does this business have a person assigned to HR/Benefits?   Yes   No
25. If Yes, are HR issues handled in-house or with a contract company. List contract company.

---

26. The business has issued an employee handbook.   Yes   No
27. Is there a written disciplinary action policy?   Yes   No
28. The company conducts new hire orientation where all company policies, procedures and rules are explained.   Yes   No
29. Employees and managers receive a copy of the rules and sign an acknowledgement form.   Yes   No
30. A back ground investigation is conducted on all new employees.   Yes   No
31. A background investigation is conducted for managers/supervisors.   Yes   No
32. Workers Compensation and customer claims are centrally reported to an assigned person and logged.   Yes   No

Our response to a "No" answer to any of these questions should be to offer the needed resources to correct the problem. Just so you know, just like outside sources are available for accounting, legal services or just about anything else needed in the way of business services, human resource experts are available too.

The last two questions relate to business safety programs. This is another area that you may not have addressed previously with your customers that is a sales opportunity of enormous proportions!

---

33. The business has a written safety policy/program in place.   Yes   No
34. Safety hazards are identified and corrected using an inspection report process.   Yes   No

---

Customer Liability and Workers Compensation claim cost is an immediate hot button for your customers. Claims costs and insurance is continuing in an upward spiral at a rate of 20% per year. You have some solutions that can be used to reign in some of these costs in the form of CCTV hardware and monitoring. We want to make you aware of the extent of the issue so you can become part of your customers' solution.

Providing solutions to high Workers Compensation through organized safety programs is one of the solutions that we make available to our customers. This effort typically reduces claims significantly, which eventually reduces insurance costs. We'd appreciate the referral!

Did you know Workers' Compensation fraud costs Americans more than $5 billion annually, threatens the jobs of Americans, and hurts employers so much that in some cases, companies go out of business or are forced to move? It adds 10 cents to every dollar of premiums. It's pervasive, growing, and often very hard to detect.

In the past several years, rising premium rates for workers' compensation insurance have increasingly pressured both insurers and employers. Despite Workers' Comp. reform legislation that has been enacted recently in states such as California, across the nation medical costs continue to grow significantly despite a decline in the number of claims filed. In a 2004 study by the National Council on Compensation Insurance (NCCI), the medical share of total benefit costs in workers' compensation rose to approximately 55 percent on a countrywide basis, with some individual state shares approaching 70 percent.

Because a significant percentage of claims start off as legitimate, Workers' Compensation fraud and abuse is hard to spot. Much of this is abuse, such as a case in which a claimant is malingering, delaying their return to work. Outright fraud is less frequent, but often costs payers dearly. The longer it takes to discover a fraudulent claim, the more money is paid out. That's why early detection of fraudulent and abusive claims is critical to containing the cost of workers' compensation. And the more insurers can decrease their losses, the more likely it is that their insurance rates will be lower as well.

Claimant fraud comes in many guises. Some workers fake injuries at the workplace to get paid for staying home. Some exaggerate the extent of injury to prolong time away from work, while others claim their injuries occurred at work, when, in fact, they happened off premises and are unrelated to work. In extreme cases, fraud is the result of organized crime, or collusion with unscrupulous doctors, therapists, and attorneys.

Organized safety inspections can identify hazards that when corrected reduce loss exposure and finally your customers can learn that the camera system that is hard to justify for crime loss is on an easy pay back track when used to dispute claims.

The opportunity for the security equipment dealer is to show their customers how various surveillance systems recording employee and customer areas can provide a substantial deterrent to false customer or employee claims. Savings can easily offset costs.

Now that you have seen what it looks like, we can talk about how to use it and how to sell it to your customers.

How do you learn how to use the survey tools? It has been our experience that once we have shown the service pro how to ask the right questions, completes the form and set up right customer files, the basis has been formed for them to start using the knowledge to establish a customer relationship that includes meaningful contributions to their customer's bottom line. We hope the explanations we have provided in this book have helped.

How can you convince your customers that they need a preventative Security Systems and Hardware Survey?

If your presence was predicated due to a crisis at the customers business, it's almost a moot point that you need to make inquiries to investigate the cause of the loss in order to recommend alternative methods to address the problem. The customer is seeking solutions to fixing a problem and preventing reoccurrence and you are providing answers. There is nothing good about a crime loss occurring, but it is a key opportunity for you to provide a valuable service to your customer that will reap many future rewards as you establish a relationship of trust.

Since much of our business is from incident driven issues that our customers experience, possessing a written plan in the form of a systems and hardware survey and a set of potential cost effective solutions right off the shelf is a powerful message that underlines the professional capacity of your service company. It is also a great satisfaction when you can tell a crime victim that you can help them solve the problem that they are experiencing.

Furthermore, the survey approach gives you a tool to use that you may need to dissuade your customer from their preconceived incorrect or incomplete analysis of what the problem is and lets you introduce the right way to solve the issue. How many times has a customer told you that they want you to fix a broken or vandalized piece of security equipment without consideration for the likelihood that it will just get broken again?

In the absence of an incident driven request for service, a number of other reasons to conduct a systems and hardware survey can be presented. If you offer preventative maintenance care for the systems you install, the loss prevention survey is a powerful tool you can use to sell your customers upgraded replacement systems for out of date or broken items that you encounter while performing routine maintenance inspections. In other words, elements of or all of the loss prevention survey can be incorporated into the preventative maintenance checklist and visa versa. It's all about asking the right questions!

Another method could be called being the "bearer of important news" to your customers. This is another way of saying that you have found out important information regarding a number of local crime events that you have heard from your police department or news sources and are concerned that you customer be aware and offer to take a look at the business to make sure that their existing security is adequate. Herein presents another reason to get to know the crime prevention people in your local police department and offer to assist them with their community outreach program.

The manner in which the survey is conducted requires thought and planning. Deciding what method to use is important in order to insure consistency at each of your customers' locations and to insure that all of the pertinent issues are covered. You don't want to have to return to a site because you forgot to check an important item on the list. So how should you conduct the survey?

What methodology works best? Inside out? Front to back? What?

Our personal preference is to start at the outer perimeter to evaluate light-ing, barriers such as fences; obvious hiding places, building vulnerabilities and critical access points from adjoining structures. Your tools will include a sketch pad for making detailed notes and a digital camera for recording the physical layout. A key part of the process requires an accurate diagram or floor plan of each site along with photographs that you will use to illustrate survey information and highlight your proposal document.

We recommend that all facility tours and surveys be conducted in the pres-ence of your customer or their management representative so that you can have the needed dialogue about the company systems and existing barriers as you go with the goal being to have uninterrupted access to the customer and their information. This is an important opportunity to find out as much as you can about your customers company, how it operates, what special problems that they have experienced and receive a clue or two you can use to weave their actual loss experience into your solutions argument.

The condition of the parking lot and lane marking is important as it repre-sents how traffic flows through the property. Good perimeter fences and simple items such as speed bumps that restrict traffic and prevent an easy escape have prevented many robberies.

Interior space should be laid out in a concentric manner for each floor of the business beginning with exit doors and the placement of windows working inward through interior passages with the center point being the place where the highest value items are kept. This usually means the safe or secure storage for high value merchandise.

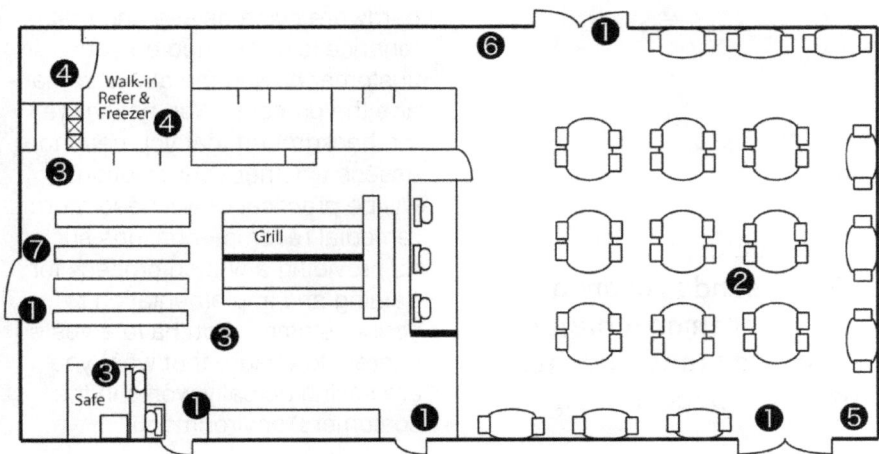

Information that you get from a survey should go beyond the scope when it is necessary to identify a proposal item that you will want to include that has not previously received consideration. An example would be to add photos and information that you observe that might include a code violation or other special consideration.

The subject of previous loss history must be surfaced during your property tour in order for you to add context to the proposal process. Whether the loss history is due to crime or claims, your proposal will be much more likely to be considered if you can clearly draw a picture matching the cost of your solution being offset by loss experience dollars and the potential recovery or prevention of future losses.

At the end of the physical tour process you will find yourself with a significant amount of information that you will use to create customer files and record profile information you will use to create your proposal and to identify future sales opportunities with that customer. Whether it is a file folder for each customer in a cabinet drawer or an electronic file on your computer is at your discretion. We think that the ability to pull out a physical file to handle and look at as well as to store all of the data on the PC fits our preference.

Our survey will save you money!

Daryl sends Amanda his crew foreman, chief job estimator (and daughter) out to do Security Surveys

With the survey information you can start to learn about and understand the impact of loss prevention policies and procedures and your proposed hardware equipment on your customers enterprise.

As we have noted, effective hardware systems use and maintenance is predicated on your customer having the ability to manage the process. You now have the background that you need to assess whether your solutions will be practical or will need more remedial recommendations such as providing a written process for training and implementation to your customer. You have a vested interest to ensure that what you are selling actually works in the customers' environment!

Determining how much on-site verbal feedback should be given at the completion of the survey is really dependant on the scope of work that needs to be included in your proposal. You should certainly let your customer know that you will need a period of time that is mutually agreeable to prepare your recommendations and avoid "shooting from the hip". Your customer should appreciate the fact that the professional recommendations that they have asked for is in response to a complicated issue and warrants more than an instant response.

Logically, not all customers will want you to conduct a survey for their benefit (go figure!). However, a lot of survey information includes the things that you need for your customer files so it makes a lot of sense to make sure each customer file has a completed set of equipment and system surveys.

Door Inspection Checklist

Customer: Date:	Comply Y/N	Condition OK/R/NA	Inspector Comment
ANSI Strike			
Butt Hinges			
Standard Bearing			
Std. Ball Bearing			
Hvy Ball Bearing			
Deadbolts			
Door Closer			
ADA Code Compliant			
Door Hold Open			
Door Stop			
Door Viewer			
Door Wind Chain			
Electric Eye			
Electric Strikes			
Electro Magnet			
Exit Alarm			
Filler Plates			
Fingersafe Guard			
Fire-Rated Exit Device			
Flush Bolts			
Full Length Hinge			
Grade 1 Lever			
Grade 2 Lever			
Grade 3 Lever			
Keyed Cylinders			
Latch Protector			
Panic Device			
Power Closer			
Push & Pull Bars			
Push & Pull Handles			
Push & Pull Lever			
Push & Pull Paddle			
Push Button Locks			
Signs			
Stand-Alone EAC			
Surface Hinge Kit			
Surface Mounted			
Threshold			
Weatherstrip			

You can keep it simple to start with and advance as needed to some of the more sophisticated methods. A few examples are offered here and many more examples are available.

Facility Security Hardware Survey©

Name of Company:	Primary Address:	Primary Contact:	Phone: E-mail
Inspection Location:	Business Type:	Address:	Date/Time:

Diagram a facility floor plan showing and identifying locations of all exterior doors, interior doors, windows, safes, cameras and other hardware components. List all items needing repair or replacement, label item, identify location and photograph for report.

Exception Report: List all items requiring replacement (RT) or repair (RP) - Complete 1 page per floor

Item:	Type/Brand/Size/LHorRH	List Location:
Door Hinges:		
Pivots: Closers:		
Electric Locking Devices:		
Mechanical Locking Devices:		
Strike Plates:		
Filler Plates:		
Kick Plates:		
Latch Guards:		
Thresh Holds:		
Door Chains:		
Door Stops:		
Garages:		
Chemical Storage:		
Equip. Storage:		
CCTV:		
Alarms:		
Safes:		
Other:		

©2006 Security Wise Group LLC

How long should you take as a time line for completion of the analysis and proposal? Again, the time frame needs to be mutually agreed upon and with all issues with customer relations; it is better to under promise and over deliver!

Chapter 4   Preventative Maintenance Programs

Sales Growth Without More Capital Investment!

Many dealers have told us that they are busier than ever but struggling to stay ahead of prior years sales volume and net profit as a percentage of sales. Working harder, less profit? You have to ask yourself...

Are you stuck in the paradigm #1 business model generating almost all sales volume from the telephone and the service shop and showroom?" Are you hopping from call to call driven by the customer call chronology? Getting a lot of "emergency" calls from regular customers needing service "right now"?

Do you take the opportunity after every repair call to suggestive sell your other services?

Do you advise your customers after an emergency call that it is more cost effective for their business to not have lock and hardware emergencies that can disrupt their business and their safety and security when it can all be avoided with your preventative maintenance plan? Do you need a better approach to providing more opportunities to grow your security business by leveraging the relationships that you already have with your existing customer base?

Preventative Maintenance Program Benefits

What's in it for your regular customers?

The customer receives an on-site inspection of all of the categories of security equipment that you sell and or service along with your recommendations regarding the phased replacement of worn items to be included in the PM program. Items to be phased in join the hardware schedule when replacement is complete.

Once you have installed a Grade 1 lockset or other equipment item, the recurring payment for your PM program covers periodic routine maintenance, repair or replacement without additional cost and is in effect an extended warranty for the agreed upon life of the item/contract. Exceptions are made for damage due to abuse, severe weather, crime or vandalism.

The customer experiences significantly lower frequency of disruption due to security equipment failure and are not charged even for emergency parts or repair unless the written exception occurs. No overtime or weekend charges, no surprises, the cost of security hardware equipment maintenance is spread throughout the fiscal year as a budgeted line item. Likewise, hardware items to be replaced are included in the customer's capital budget and paid for as a capital expenditure with the cost spread over the anticipated life of the item.

What's in it for you?

Your on-site inspection provides you with a sales opportunity to let your customers know that they should be replacing worn or outdated hardware on a prioritized basis before the need for emergency repair and disruption occurs. You gain control by scheduling repair and replacement during regular periodic maintenance visits called for in the contract. (More sales = more profit).

You schedule the service at your discretion during off times instead of peak busy times of the month during a day-part agreed upon by you and your customer. Maybe evening or other non-typical business hours makes sense as long as it does not incur overtime. Plus you can fit this customer into the same geographical area as other customers and save gas and windshield time! (Less overhead = more profit)

Regular recurring payment means your are not always waiting for your customers accounting systems to review and approve every invoice before payment can be generated often taking 60 or 90 days. (= improved cash flow)

Your regular presence in your customers business positions you to allow your relationship to evolve into the new paradigm business model providing even more loss preventions services such as proactive survey and service programs. (More sales + overhead savings + regular cash flow = more profit!)

We can illustrate the use of the sale of PM contracts to increase the gross and net sales of a retrofit security pro business just like yours. Our fictitious example we will call LPSolutions Group does business in a mid-sized city and provides locksmith service and has recently expanded the business to include digital CCTV, electronic access control and security alarm systems.

A customer of LPSG, Gordo's Fast Food Restaurant is a 54-seat restaurant, part of a twelve-store chain featuring Southwest American food in a shopping center lot located in front of a large home improvement store in a commercial neighborhood. A four-lane highway connects the shopping center to a major interstate highway located a mile away. The Gordo's chain has been in business twenty years and has experienced a few robberies over the years and a half dozen serious deposit thefts and periodically has internal control issues that drives a high food cost variance.

The restaurant owner, Gordo Chance, readily agreed to have LPSG survey the restaurants and recommend security improvements to improve loss and cost controls.   Each of the Gordo's Restaurants are physically identical and have original lock equipment that is a Grade 2 import at best and camera systems that do exist are outdated and use VCR's to record store activities. The store alarm system is outdated and the contract with the old service provider has expired and will not be renewed.

Looking at the store floor plan, you have recommended equipment placement that looks like the following two illustrations. The first plan shows alarm equipment placement. Front and back door locksets have been retrofitted to a Grade 1 lockset with door closers also upgraded to heavy-duty commercial specifications.

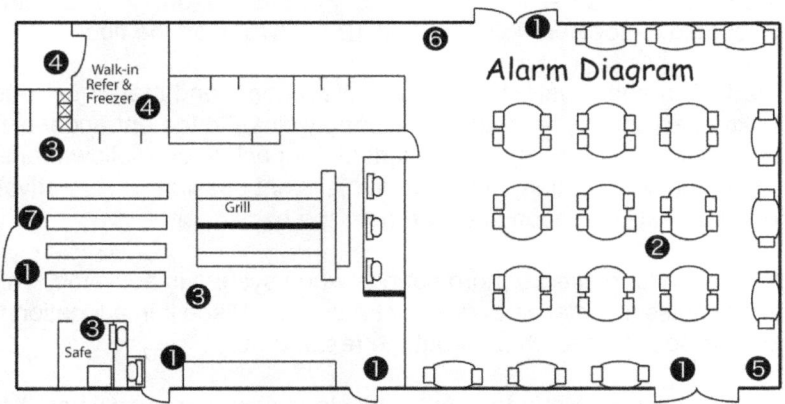

Alarm Diagram

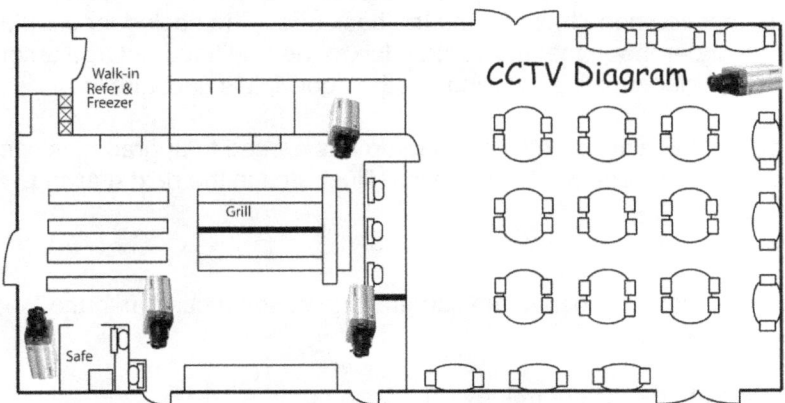

CCTV Diagram

1. Door and window contact switches - Open doors or windows and alarm sounds. The store perimeter doors and windows all have contact switches. The system allows the manager to set the system in "stay" mode for late night business that arms the doors but bypasses the drive through windows and motion sensors.

2. Strobe light - Strobe pulses when alarm is set off to alert police and others with a bright pulsing light.

3. Passive infrared sensors - Sense heat and movement and alarm sounds. By requiring both heat and motion to activate, false alarms are reduced.

4. Hold up alarm switches - Press or pull and silent alarm is activated. Our experience with restaurant robberies shows that many times robbers force employees into the walk in before making their escape. During the robbery, employees are often told to stay in the walk-in and sometimes the employees are tied up or otherwise restrained. For this reason, hold up alarm switches should be located no more than 12-18 inches off the floor.

5. Key Pad - Turns the system on and off. We recommend that where possible the key pad should be located reasonably close to the entrance/exit of the store and also have direct line of sight of the back door to allow manager control of the back door alarm function. If this is not possible, it is relatively inexpensive to install a second keypad near the back door.

6. Siren/Horn - A loud siren or horn sounds when system is activated. This high decibel noise is installed to disorient a burglar. Place it in a location to maximize the sound effect throughout the restaurant.

7. Local alarm/Chime - Sounds a noticeably loud chime or buzz when the back door is opened. The purpose of the back door alarm is to alert the manager that someone has opened the back door. The back door should always be under the managers control due to the likelihood of large amounts of food and other supplies "walking out the door" if it is uncontrolled.

In addition to the alarms and locks, Gordo has agreed to upgrade his camera systems with placement of hardware illustrated in the next drawing.

Coverage includes the following locations:

1. Dining Room - Purpose of the camera is to observe customer and front counter activity.

2. Front Counter - Covers money transactions.

3. Drive -Thru - Covers both back register cash and front window food delivery.

4. Back Door - Covers both the walk-in refrigerators and the back door to monitor employee activity.

Note that additional options may include the Managers office and exterior applications such as the parking lot and drive thru lanes.

5. System includes 125 GB DVR, flat panel monitors for the front line and the managers office. Plastic domes to prevent tampering and damage from environmental contamination protect all cameras. External access is by IP protocols using high speed DSL.

The cost of the system improvements LPSG will invoice Gordo's for parts and labor will be as follows:

Door Hardware: (Brand Name)

Two pairs of front doors including closers and new crash bar hardware retro-fitted to the existing aluminum framed glass doors.

One back door crashbar set retrofitted to existing steel back door with heavy-duty door closer hardware.

Door Closers Aluminum Door	260.00 ea. x 4 = $1,040
Exit Devices Aluminum Door	520.00 ea x 4 = $2,080
Door Closer Metal Door	260.00 ea x 1 = $260
Exit Devices	429.00 ea x 1 = $429
Labor:	@95 x 8 Hrs = $750
Sub Total: $4,559	x 12 locations = $54,708

Security Alarm System Installed:
Sub Total: $ 1,550.00 x 12 locations = $18,600

Recurring cost of monitoring is $25 per month x 12 locations = $300 or

$3,600.00 per year.
(Note: Central station monitoring charge is $6 per month per location)

Camera System:

5 Cameras in dome housing, office monitor and frontline monitor with 125GB DVR with remote dial in capability and DVD writer.

Sub Total Installed: $6,500.00 x 12 locations = $78,000.00

You Do The Math...

Grand Total of installed equipment and labor for Gordo's 12 restaurants: $151,308.00

Typical Preventative Maintenance contract is 10% of the value of the hardware per year or $15,130

Each quarterly service call to your customers' locations = $315 EACH...

There is an alternative way of looking at service. A significant number of dealers that we talk to have been very successful taking care of existing customer service by offering service membership discounts for all labor when a service call is requested. Membership fees are another form of recurring income!

From the customer point of view, big dollar security systems might be a hard sell and you may want to surface some finance considerations. For many businesses, leasing property may have significant financial benefits:

Leasing is less capital intensive than purchasing, so if a business has constraints on its capital, it can grow more rapidly by leasing property than it could by purchasing the property outright. Capital assets may fluctuate in value. Leasing shifts risks to the lessor, but if the property market has shown steady growth over time, a business that depends on leased property is sacrificing capital gains.

Leasing may provide more flexibility to a business, which expects to grow or move in the relatively short term, because a lessee is not usually obliged to renew a lease at the end of its term. Depreciation of capital assets has different tax and financial reporting treatment from ordinary business expenses. Lease payments are considered expenses, which can be set off against revenue when calculating taxable profit at the end of the relevant tax accounting period.

There can some significant drawbacks:

If circumstances dictate that a business must change its operations significantly, it may be expensive or other-wise difficult to terminate a lease before
the end of the term.

In some cases, a business may be able to sublet property no longer required, but this may not recoup the costs of the original lease, and, in any
event, usually requires the consent of the original lessor.

Tactical legal considerations usually make it expedient for lessees to default
on their leases. The loss of book value is small and any litigation can usually
be settled on advantageous terms. This is an improvement on the position
for those companies owning their own property. Although it can be easier for
a business to sell property if it has the time, forced sales frequently realize
lower prices and can seriously affect book value.

If the business is successful, lessors may demand higher rental payments
when leases come up for renewal. If the value of the business is tied to the
use of that particular property, the lessor has a significant advantage over
the lessee in negotiations.

Here is a list of questions that you need to answer for yourself as they relate
to your company circumstances. Each security hardware business will probably see the benefits and disadvantages when each of these questions is
answered. It comes down to "What's in it for you".

We think the questions for you to answer for yourself come down to these:

- Reasons for PM programs?
- Why should I get involved?
- Will controlling overtime labor expenses be a benefit for me?
- What are my customers' expectations related to equipment life?
- What are the real expectations of equipment life and how do I reconcile
  the two?
- What do my hardware manufacturers warrant?
- What frequency of visits for mechanical and electronic components
  should I offer?
- What products are the most and least labor intensive?
- What makes the most sense for your market place, recurring income
  from a PM Program or "Membership" programs with small monthly

fees and discounted service rates. Which is best?

* How would I identify new sales opportunities with each PM visit?
* What pre-inspection dialog should I have with my customer?
* How much of a post inspection dialog should you have?
* What should be on my PM report and recommendations?
* Who will follow up on recommendations you make on the PM inspection report?
* What are some billing considerations? Bill accompanies the report?
* Should I consider subcontracting inspection services? Create a position?
* What training and expertise should the inspector have to perform a PM inspection?
* Should my legal counsel conduct a legal review?

These are some of the many questions that you should ask. We think that if you plan every job with a maintenance or other recurring income feature to present to your customer, you will add value to the relationship!

Meanwhile down at Joe's a
customer walks in...two keys cut and a
bottle of water!

Daryl figures out that all of that price
discounting is killing his bottom line.
He is working harder for less profit!

Chapter 5   Putting Together Your Recommendations

A number of tasks surface as you prepare to create a customer proposal. First of all is the task to collate all of your information into an orderly and consistent file for easy examination. We'll assume that you have separated all of your loss prevention and hardware surveys along with your site sketches and notes by location and have printed out the photos that you took, labeled and filed them also by location.

In his book "The 7 Habits Of Highly Effective People", Stephen Covey recommends a number of important factors that can influence planning and how successful your enterprise will be.

He starts his list of habits with being "Proactive" and finishes with a process that essentially ends with a habit of continual learning and improvement that he calls "Sharpening the saw". Most importantly he advises two intermediate tasks that include "Begin with the end in mind" and "First things first." The point is to visualize the end result that you want to achieve and list an order of importance to the needed tasks.

With that in mind, think about what might be included in your hardware and service package that the survey tour experience established in your mind and list the hardware components likely to be included in the end result.

We like this approach as a starting point because being able to step back at the beginning of the project to take a mental snapshot of the physical and cultural components of your customers business can give you a clearer "Big Picture" impression of how the overall components may or may not fit in before you dive into the minutia of pages of hardware lists, specifications and applications needed at the various customer facilities. It can also shape your thought process regarding what type of system components will integrate into the whole and what tools will need to be in place to manage the system.

The "First things first" process can relate to identifying the most critical security issues that you found and determine an appropriate list of alternative measures that can be used to address the problem. For instance, you may have found that the broken locks that you were called in to repair, only represents the leading edge to the impending collapse of your customers key control system due to degraded and obsolete locksets and a lack of key control policies to insure accountability.

You may find it cost effective to propose a stand alone or even centrally controlled electronic access control system controlled by you is superior to replacing all of the mechanical hardware and still be without long term control due to the customers historical problem with administering the keys. Beyond establishing the criticality list, concern and care should be given to prioritizing hardware and systems implementation processes.

Few small to midsized companies are going to be able to handle the change process from poor old security practices to the new effective requirements without a significant amount of preparation and project management assistance. Keep in mind the need to phase in the program since you should not assume that just because it was working when you finished the job, it would be able to continue to perform without system maintenance and management.

As you plan the proposal, consider another Covey habit, which is to think "Win/Win". Here we see the need to create empathy with your customers needs and concerns that may include the distinct possibility found in many companies of a degree of technophobia. You may find that a solution to a customers' loss exposure that is very obvious to you, is simply not understood by the people expected to make it work! It explains the fact that when touch screen registers were first introduced in fast food restaurants, some found it necessary to replace product words with pictures on the screen.

We experienced this issue in the process of installing digital video recording equipment for a CCTV application in a company a few years ago. As most of you recall, video recording in the form of a VCR was pretty widely grasped by most people eventually and pretty much everybody had one at home and could put in a movie and play it. Remember, however, lots of owners never figured out how to set the clock which simple flashed on "12:00" all day nor did they figure out how to record a program. Most of the people operating the equipment understood that the store VCR tapes had to be changed every 8 hours, but almost nobody did.

You may also recall, the initial advent of the digital revolution included a transition stage where upon the analogue picture captured by the camera was converted to a digital signal by a device called a "Multiplexer" which was still recorded on tape, but could provide a clearer image, recorded longer periods of time and could be played back as a single frame or on multiple screens. Tapes no longer needed to changed but every 24 hours but still did not get changed!

Unfortunately, playback was complicated since every manufacturer had their own proprietary recording play-back scheme and the tapes could no longer be played in any VCR, only in a recorder attached to the right multiplexer. The days of the user friendly VCR were over and resulted in a reduced usage of the technology, which was deemed way too difficult to use without some training and a pretty good short instruction sheet.

DVR equipment was not a whole lot friendlier at first but eventually proprietary-encoding schemes began to be replaced with Internet protocol systems that could be accessed either on-site or remotely.

So Think "Win/Win" describes an attitude whereby mutually beneficial solutions are sought, that satisfy the needs of oneself as well as others, or, in the case of a conflict, both parties involved.

Covey warns that giving out advice before having empathetically understood a person and their situation will likely result in that advice being rejected. Thoroughly listening to another person's concerns instead of reading out your own autobiography is purported to increase the chance of establishing a working communication. He terms it "Seek First to Understand, Then to be understood".

Collating information from completed surveys is a process of identifying risk exposure due to missing or insufficient barriers or processes. The categories of information are important to establish the relationship between the exposure needing correction and the solutions that you can provide to solve the problem or reduce loss potential.

A key element to the process is to determine what current losses your customer is experiencing. This can be tough since you will often find business owners are reluctant to share this information unless you are at the customers' place of business because you have been called to deal with the aftermath of a loss incident. If you can quantify how often similar incidents are occurring at the customers business locations, say for the last five years, you can begin to show the impact of losses over a longer range and be able to start the process of developing a proposal with a return on investment strategy.

A lot of the security expenditures of small and midsized companies are incident driven and your ability to analyze and assess the real proximate cause of your customers losses can give you a big boost toward maximizing your sales. For multi-unit customers, this can mean an opportunity to not only establish security measures at the location of the loss but at the other customer business units as well.

It is helpful to picture in your mind that a loss event that your customer experiences is likely the "tip of the ice-berg". Typically large theft losses, for instance, are not a big bolt out of the blue occurrence but rather the result of internal control conditions that have allowed many lesser crime incidents to occur prior to the "big loss". The big loss occurs when a pattern of small thefts by a crooked employee progress into larger losses due to greed. So below the tip of the iceberg, under water so to speak, is the much larger pattern of smaller loss incidents that perhaps have gone unnoticed or at least unresolved by the business management.

The challenge is to show your customers how to attack the base problem and not just put a band-aid on the visible issue. You can show your customer that your service goes beyond a new set of keys or hanging a camera on the wall. Your skills include offering comprehensive loss prevention services and that's a really powerful asset to your customers!

The basic problem is to determine how do you go about assessing shrinkage loss impact in real dollars that your customer is experiencing and may not be addressing in the right way?

We have often heard a business owner tell us that he believes that someone is stealing from him but they just can't catch them. They have assumptions about who may be stealing but cannot prove it. They do know that when they balance beginning and ending inventory versus the sales numbers, they cannot find a percentage of the inventory. It's gone. It may well be between three to five percent of your customers gross sales!

Some of your customers will not tell you what their shrinkage percentage is and others simply may not really know. The fall back position you can take is to simply present you justification arguments using published industry average numbers.

For instance, not long ago the Food Marketing Institute polled their grocery store customers and determined on average that markets are losing 3% of their net sales to theft. About 43% from employee theft, 35% to shoplifters and the rest to delivery shortages and fraud. This on an industry with a razor thin 1½% profit margin!

What source or methods can you use for getting industry segment data? We have found that most business enterprises have advocacy organizations like FMI. They are usually found at association websites or in various trade journals that are published in print that you can find in your local library or on line. Typically, your customer knows if they are above or below the average for their industry once you have shown them and will do the math on their own as you relate the average potential profit recovery.

The amount of money they are losing is sitting on the table. Your small business customer can walk away without it or can invest in equipment, policies and procedures to pay for it all from recovered profit dollars like the big companies do. The loss impact to your end user customers profit picture creates cost justification for hardware capital expense.

Another consideration you face while creating your recommendations is what do you do when you identify important needed services that you don't provide? Included here is what installations can you sub-contract if you don't have the expertise or do not have the resources to complete an obviously needed component of the plan? You can identify sub-contractor sources and simply include the work in your proposal. Building contractors do this every day. Need an electrician? Hire one.

There are many legal considerations to consider while preparing recommen-dations. Beyond the local code compliance issues, you should consider the proposal recommendations must meet the variety of new governmental and non-governmental standards that are continuously emerging so that recom-mendations meet or exceed expectations of performance that we discussed earlier in the book.

If your survey identified lots of missing policies and procedures you might be asking yourself, "Now what"? For many of you, recommending policies and procedures to your customers is new territory. The recurring theme of this book as well as our previous ones is the following premise:

From the end users perspective, "an effective loss prevention program is a variety of hardware tools that are managed by a series of rules, policies and procedures. All entities must be designed to work together to make the program work".

Look at it this way. As a technically oriented person working in a technical field, you have a high degree of confidence that the equipment you install in your customers business will reliably work. For instance, the camera system and DVR you installed worked perfectly and you trained a manager or owner how it works and you left behind a manual and walked out of the door. You may have even sold the owner on a maintenance program and will return periodically to make sure it continues to work and gets a tune-up. End of job, right? Not from the end users perspective.

Your end user may well be a non-technical person working in a non-techni-cally oriented business. Without a comprehensive written instruction how the camera equipment, for instance, must be used to work as a crime pre-vention tool for the business, it will eventually become a decoration on the wall. A written policy statement will not only instruct the managers how the equipment works but will list practices and procedures that will be used by the company to insure effective use of their loss prevention tools.

A typical policy will state the managers responsibility to use the equipment properly for the intended purpose, instruct how to extract evidentiary video, what procedures to use when requests are received from law enforcement pursuant to a loss investigation and a number of other considerations to insure the consistent use of the equipment in order for the evidence to hold up under legal and court scrutiny.

We are putting together a presentation!

The process of tying polices and procedures to hardware use and maintenance is most reliably completed by experts such as Certified Protection Professionals. Once you have established that your customer needs policies and procedures to insure the proper use of the equipment and you can pass on the cost of a professional resource to write and implement the policies for your customer, the CPP in essence, becomes another subcontractor that you can use. It's just like hiring an electrician!

An equally Win/Win approach is to be able to offer to your customers some basic policies that you can hand to your customer. We have included some basic policies at our website for your use. It is very effective, for instance when you have installed a new retrofit lock

Amanda completed a security survey at King Happy Foods and an outline of AAA Security recommendations was developed!

system to be able to hand your customer a copy of a key control procedure at the end of an installation during the use training process. It is the touch of a professional to provide additional levels of service not expected. Also to be considered as part of your recommendation presentations are potential recurring costs. Examples might include alarm monitoring, built in PM/service programs, key/user changes and cost of emergency service. Obviously the more recurring services you can provide benefits your sales volume and cash flow and you can argue the benefits to the end user in reducing emergency call frequency and resulting overtime for both of you.

Your customers policies, procedures and company
rules can make or break your security hardware plan!

Chapter 6   Proposals That Sell Themselves

There are many different approaches to creating a proposal that can be used to explain to your customer all of the products and benefits to the program that you recommend. Among the considerations that you must be aware of is that the type and detail of the proposal needs to match the scope of the job and clearly state the benefits of each type of item and service to your customers identified need.

The proposal paints the big picture of what goods and services that your customer can expect, what it looks like, what it's for and how it all ties together. The proposal key is the information that was obtained on the SWG® and/or Hardware Survey forms that you have completed.

The construction of the proposal should have a number of the following section dividers to facilitate organization of the document.

1.   Title Page

2.   Table of Contents

3.   Introduction or "Executive Summary"

4.   "Who We Are" performance qualifications summary

5.   Technical Proposal

6.   Bill of Materials

7.   Installation, Implementation and Maintenance Support

8.   Terms and Conditions

9.   Appendix

Clearly a very large scale job ($$$$) will require significant detailed information while smaller facilities ($$) may only involve a few pages and illustrations. In our view, "keep it simple" when ever possible is the key to a successful proposal.

The Title Page should list the customers name, the document title and any restrictions that you need to place regarding how the proposal information can be used. Obviously, you would prefer that your customer not use your carefully crafted proposal listing your well-reasoned equipment specifications, cost benefit analysis and your company pricing as a tool for the customer to shop the best price around town.

While you may not be able to prevent it, you can at least notify all who look at the document that the proposal has been submitted in confidence and contains trade secrets and/or privileged commercial or financial information. Those that are inclined to misuse your proprietary proposal document will be on notice that what they are doing is unethical.

A personal touch we like to see is to apply the customers' company logo on the title page if it is available to let them know that you respect their company image. You can often pluck a usable copy from the customers website!

The Table of Contents should not be merely a list of the title of each proposal section. It is the page that you need to use to grab the attention and interest of the reader! Each section title should tell the reader what is included, what the solution will do for them and more! Add some excitement by not just calling it the "Proposal for Jones Hardware"; instead title it "Major cost savings solutions for Jones Hardware". The idea is to inject a sense of urgency and ownership into the process.

The "Executive Summary" or "Introduction" Should contain a brief outline regarding the contents of the proposal, how it was developed and why it represents a cost effective solution to the identified loss exposure issues raised with the completion of the loss prevention and hardware surveys. Inject the notion to start saving money now!

This is a good place to discuss broad stroke implications of the exposure created by missing systems, policies and procedures. Using real loss numbers from your customer as well as those typical of the customers industry can be especially effective when stating the cost saving value of the proposal. Urgency calls for the enumeration of what losses are occurring every single day.

The "Who Are We" section performs the task of describing your company's capability as a professional service systems integration firm fully experienced at fulfilling a vast number of customized loss prevention solutions. They need to know that you are going to solve their problem. Your customer may not be aware of all of the types of services that you can perform for them and now is the time to tell them.

The listing of business references and the names of former or current clients belong here and allow you to list each service in your Toolbox and what the benefit to your customer is.

The Technical Proposal section is the core of the proposal and here you will list exactly what products you will be installing in the customers facility. List important product features that your customer will be able to use and why the item is important in the overall loss prevention picture. Paste a picture of the item into the proposal; state the model and brand name of the manufacturer *only* if the customer requires it in any published bid specification and reference further information such as the specification in the Bill Of Materials section. Illustrate where it is going to go in the customer's facility using a floor plan diagram.

The Technical Proposal should tie directly to quoted sections of the loss prevention and hardware surveys that serve as a basis of the proposal. Here's where you are stating your solutions to your customers missing hardware, policies and procedures.

The Bill Of Materials section merely lists the technical specifications of the equipment to be installed. The idea is to make the Bill Of Materials as generic as possible to prevent the customer from performing a line item comparison with other vendors as well as to allow you to substitute products of equal or better than the original specification. For instance, instead of listing the manufacturer and model number of the UPS system or cameras, we would list our company as the manufacturer of some items.

The Installation, Implementation and Maintenance section tells the story of how you plan to put it all together. Your customer wants to know how long will it take, will it impact his business activity and how will he and his key employees learn how to use it all. Your customer will want to know all about what to do if something is not working correctly and how to get the problem quickly resolved.

This is where you lay out the details and benefits of your Preventative Maintenance Program!

The Terms and Conditions section is about the money! By now, if you have done your job, your customer is focused on the cost of not proceeding rather than the cost to fix the problem because you have provided all of the return on investment arguments needed to overcome objections.

You will state the deposit amount needed to commence scheduling any progress payments and final payment due upon receipt of the invoice. List warranty information, owner provided items such as electrical work, mounting space and fees taxes and documentation. You may wish to state that penalties apply to late payments.

And finally a proposal acceptance page signed by the customer and your company representative.

A last optional item is the Document Appendix that can contain reference letters, access control system literature, news articles and corporate brochures.

So those are some of our thoughts about the proposal content. But, of course, that is not the final answer because every one of you has your own unique presentation script that may touch the whole spectrum from informal verbal to bound copy and indexed formal proposals.

The real question is does it achieve the primary goal. Does it sell your services and products to your desired customer base? If not, the obvious question you have to ask yourself is "Why Not"?

Answer the following questions about your current approach. Are you missing any key communications elements that can help you close the deal? Does your proposal contain so much "legalese" language that the customer thinks that they have to run the whole thing past their attorney before they proceed? Are you saying too little or too much?

What document appearance and content are you using now?

Are you using customer logos or other identifiers to tap into the customers company identity and culture?

Are you using visual photos and illustrations of generic proposed equipment versus lengthy written narrative?

Are you using site photos from your customers business to illustrate locations and use of hardware versus narrative?

Are you using your diagrams prepared at each site to illustrate different issues and installations?

Are you including a convincing return on investment argument based on available based on the customers stated loss history? Can you illustrate how recovery of 1-2% of losses will pay for the investment?

Are you addressing the importance of missing policies and procedures?

Are you tying in the missing policies and procedures needed to manage existing and proposed systems?

Are you introducing how to create and implement management policies using the resources available from your company to the customer?

How should you show priority of creation and installation of policies, procedures and barriers? Time line? Priority listing? Other?

What is the method you use as the best way to show cost of equipment? Cost per year of expected life of the item for each operating unit? Monthly cost per unit? Other?

Do you routinely introduce alternative financing such as leasing to illustrate the actual monthly cost of equipment per the customers operating unit?

Do you always have a fallback plan to phase in recommendations using customers own timetable?

How are your strategies for overcoming sticker shock?

How do you explain exclusions and disclaimers?

Have you gotten a legal review of your proposal content from your own attorney?

**"Return on investment" is
what your customer wants to hear!**

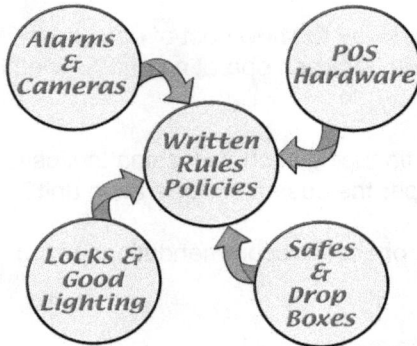

Daryl knows:
"An effective loss prevention program consists of
a variety of hardware tools that are managed by a
series of rules, policies and procedures".

Daryl Shows the King Happy Food Folks what he has in mind to help them reduce their shrinkage!

Chapter 7   Presenting Your Proposal

Presentations

Many people reading this book may not have had extensive practice at program presentations or public speaking. In truth, a one-on-one sales presentation should be planned like any other public speaking engagement. For that reason, in this chapter, we have mined the depths of information about what is being said about creating and delivering presentations and of course include our own experience.

Initial planning for your proposal presentation.

This is where you begin to tailor the talk to the situation, and for that reason this stage is very important for a successful presentation. In Chapter 3 we addressed finding out what your customer really wants through a process of interviewing, discussion and use of the survey tools. You have gained insight into how and where the customer has the greatest exposure to losses and what types of losses have already occurred historically. You may even want to do a literature search on your customer's business type to identify areas of common interest and issues experienced by the customers industry as a whole.

Since you have developed a loss profile of your customer, your planning process can now center on being able to explain to your customer exactly what you are going to do for them in a clear and concise presentation. If you have done your homework, you now have a pretty good idea of what keeps your customer awake at night (or should be keeping him awake!) So you are now about to develop your theme for the presentation.

For instance, based on your survey process and interviews with the customer, you have determined that the customer is experiencing significant inventory losses from the stock supply warehouse. This concern surfaced as the highest concern of the moment to your customer. Your theme for the presentation will address the issue to solve the immediate problem. It may not make the most sense to start your presentation by telling your customer that you think a camera installation at another site should be his top priority – even though it may be the true solution to the problem!

While the current customer problem focus may well be just a symptom of the real problem, you none-the-less want to address their primary issue first. As you build credibility, you may notice a lot less resistance to your analysis of the real problem. If you approach other issues initially you may be swimming upstream in order to explain how your solution seemingly in a different direction can solve the customers immediate problem.   So the best approach may well be to start at the customers central concern and work your way out to the real issue which will then can be woven around the current "reference" issue that was described as a warehouse inventory loss.

As you begin preparing the presentation, you'll need to determine a few logistical parameters such as the form of the delivery you will be making. Will this be an informal chat, a discussion, or a more formal presentation with audio-visual or PowerPoint presentation? How many people are expected to attend the presentation?

Many businesses will want a number of their people to hear what you have to say and you want an interactive audience. Try to pick a venue that prevents outside distractions and gives you enough space to show and tell your program. That means that for complex projects, you will need a meeting or conference room but a small proposal may just need a table at the local diner.

You also need to determine if there is a time allotment for the presentation. The longer you have to talk, the more freedom you will have to explore the topic. If only a short time is allotted you need to be very clear and need to address the topic directly with a minimum of peripheral discussion.

You will be presenting some novel concepts to your customer audience and hopefully be building upon their prior knowledge. Either way, make sure you cover the basics clearly, and early in the talk, to avoid losing the audience.

Preparation

Once you have a clear idea of what you want to say, you'll have to decide how to say it. Unlike a conversation or a written document, your talk is a one-shot attempt to make a point. By contrast, a conversation consists of repetitions and clarifications based on questions and immediate feedback, while a written paper allows a reader to puzzle through its contents as often as necessary. It is essential that your presentation be well constructed and tidy, and that your points be presented in both a logical sequence and unambiguously. This all takes a fair amount of preparation and you will likely be less successful if you "wing it".

Start preparing far in advance by thinking through what needs to be said. Assemble your proposal materials and have a professional document to hand to your customer. You have collected and assembled visual aid material, which relates to the topic from the unusual sources such as manufacturers catalogs and websites and your plan will include a sequence when you conduct your "show and tell". The final product will be more fully developed and interesting.

We have a few thoughts about your preparation.

Using big letters and a bold pen, write a clear statement of the problem and its importance, and then pin that statement on the wall above your desk. Develop this theme into one jargon-free sentence that will catch the attention of the customer. Next, identify the issues you plan to address.

Arrange these issues in a logical sequence (which may change as you develop the talk). This process is easier if you use index cards to organize your talk, with one idea per card.

Computer-based presentation programs (such as PowerPoint) can be time-savers. These programs are good tools for organizing your presentation (an electronic version of the index cards idea), they can be used to create visuals for the presentation (e.g., slides and transparencies), and even project those visuals during the presentation. Remember, however, these tools are most effective using a large screen projection or a large flat panel monitor.

You should only consider running the program on a laptop if you are presenting one-on-one with your customer and have given a lot of thought to what will be useful to the explanation rather than a distraction such as spreadsheets or small font descriptions. Think BIG type size or just use it to show pictures of the components you want to install.

You should avoid using lists (First ..., Second ...); you may confuse listing systems or you may discover later in the talk that you've missed a point entirely, and then you'll be forced to backtrack. Both of these problems tend to distract your audience away from the points you are trying to make, and both give the appearance of poor organizational skills.

Retention of information by the audience is reduced as a talk proceeds, so if you do want to make a series of points, organize them from the most important topic of concern that you have discovered to be your customers top priority to their least stated important priority. That way, the audience is more likely to remember the important points later.

Determine transition elements, which will help your audience to follow the link from one issue to the next. These should be logical, and may presented by posing a question, or explaining your own discovery of the link's existence. For instance, a discussion of how installing a camera system can impact employee theft issues and can segue into a discussion of why missing policies and procedures can be upgraded and included to complete the package needed to manage the hardware tools.

Keep it simple. Use short sentences with simple constructions and the sentence structure is more similar to normal speaking styles. Run through the talk once and think about what the presentation sequence is. This is the time to discard nonessential items.

You really should not assume that your customer will know anything about basic concepts that form the foundation of your presentation. Define any basic concepts early in the presentation and avoid buzzwords and jargon.

Think about potential questions that your presentation raises and come up with the answers before your audience can. Prepare thumbnails sketches of your visual aids, and then run through the talk again. As you create the essential visual aids don't forget to proofread! Do so while there is plenty of time to reprint that critical slide so that you can correct any with glaring typos!

When in doubt about which presentation medium to use choose the format, which is the least complex, which remains consistent with both clarity and content of the presentation. Keep in mind that the more technology you use, the more things can go wrong. Nothing is more embarrassing than the pause that occurs when your computer quits or the projector bulb burns out! The Simple-Stupid method of describing a lockset that you want to install may most effectively be presented by handing the customer an example of the actual lock to handle. This allows you to point and describe the features as your customer focuses on how the lock looks and feels.

If you do need to use multimedia technology in your presentation, call ahead to make sure the technology you require is supported in the room where you'll be talking!

The most important preparation factor is to REHEARSE!

Some of us like to just quietly practice in an empty room and some of the bolder-older presenters actually videotape themselves to self-critique their performance. This can be a very humbling and sobering experience. Many professional presenters say that they practice each presentation at least ten times before the actual delivery!

Remember, the shorter the talk, the more difficult it will be to cover the material clearly and completely. Be strict about including only what is essential information for the presentation, and removing all the non-essential tidbits.

You can save any chit-chat if you have time at the end of the presentation.

Important Elements

Keeping these elements in mind as you prepare and practice the presentation will reduce the amount of re-working you'll have to do as it evolves, and will result in a more streamlined and effective end product.

Rate:

The optimal rate for a presentation is said to be fewer than a 100 words per minute. Any faster and the audience can't absorb the additional information. Use pauses, and repeat critical information. On the other hand, if your presentation is too slow, your audience may try to speed up the delivery in not too subtle ways like filling in words for you before you can say them! Find the happy medium for your current audience.

Opening:

The opening should catch the interest and attention of the audience immediately. Start with a short sentence telling them exactly why you are there such as "I have reviewed your information and have prepared a plan for you to recover a substantial amount of profit while doing a better job of protecting your people and property".

Transitions:

The link between successive elements of the proposal should be planned. You should make the relation between the different components of the proposed plan clear to the audience.

Conclusion:

Summarize the main elements of the proposal and show them how each element ties into the profit recovery plan and how each will extend the protection of the customers' assets. This is where you tie in the return on their investment.

Length:

If you have been given a time limit, be realistic regarding what you can achieve in a short period of time. If you simply cannot present the necessary elements of the proposal without running over, try to renegotiate for a more adequate later date or time frame. In any case, if you do agree to a short time frame for your presentation, don't run overtime!   You can shorten your talk by removing details, concepts, and information, not by eliminating words. If it becomes absolutely essential to supply details, rely on your written proposal and follow up, if necessary, to close the deal.

Remember that there is no point in giving a presentation if the audience isn't listening. It is always appropriate to use techniques to retain audience interest, provided these techniques don't detract from the content or professionalism of the talk. Equipment parts and items to handle can often spike interest.

Having spent all that time preparing the talk itself, there are still a few things you can do at the last minute, which will help ensure a successful presentation. Or, if you are the nervous type, help fill time.

If possible, take a tour the place that you'll be using for the presentation ahead of time. If you are doing an audio visual or PowerPoint presentation in a meeting room for a larger group, look for potential problems with line of sight due to furniture, dark spots due to dead overhead lights, intruding sound from ventilation - these all can be fixed with a bit of prior warning and a polite request.

On occasion, you may need to make a proposal to customers that are not local and you have to travel to another location that may be unfamiliar to you. You have two choices. You can either drag all of your stuff with you or plan on having the necessary tools and exhibits available to you when you get there. Hauling a CD or a thumb drive with you is a whole lot easier than dragging along a laptop if you have to fly to the destination.

If you need specialized equipment, make sure it is available ahead of time - don't spring that information on your host at the last minute. It's your show, so ask for help with the equipment if you need it; it's better to ask for help then fumble around during the presentation. Determine who will be controlling equipment for you.

Computer presentations introduce a whole host of potential issues. Is the host software compatible with your presentation? Are the fonts, bullets, and colors, etc. the same? Is there a sound card in the host computer? Is the sound system operational - but not too painfully loud?

Back-up your presentation before you leave using an alternate medium, then bring it with you separately from the one you plan to use (e.g., packed in a different suitcase), or E-mail it to yourself as an attachment - you may be able to access it from your destination if needed. Alternatively, E-mail it to your host and ask that her or she download the file and test it on the computer you'll be using - BEFORE you depart for the trip!

Keep in mind that failures of technology can be devastating, but that 1) the embarrassment is greater on the part of the host if their equipment is at fault, and 2) the host is usually impressed if you provide an alternate solution to the problem suggesting you are proactive and prepared.

Handling Questions

Your presentation doesn't end once you've finished what you have to say. The questions that follow often are the part of the talk, which influences your customer the most. This is the part of the presentation where your ability to interact with the audience will be evaluated. Since you can't always predict "the what" you'll be asked, how can you prepare for the questioning? We have some suggestions:

If you are in a group situation, always repeat each question so that everyone knows what you've been asked. Before you answer, take a moment to reflect on the question. By not rushing to give an answer, you show a degree of respect for the customer, but mostly you give yourself time to be sure you are answering the question that actually was asked. If you are unsure, restate the question or ask for a clarification.

Above all, wait for the customer to finish asking the question before you begin your answer! The only exception is in a group situation when it becomes necessary to break in on a vague, rambling question; this is your show, and you have only a limited time to make your presentation. It is essential, however, that you break in tactfully. Say something like "So, are you asking ....?" This will focus the question and give you a place to begin an answer.

We hate to admit it but once in a while, you will be asked a question that you simply do not know the answer to. Don't fake it! Simply tell the customer that you don't know but will get back to them with the answer. Don't forget to follow up.

A Presentation checklist might include the following items:

*   Does the sales venue offer privacy in a neutral environment – i.e. over lunch or coffee?
*   What is the order of presentation?
*   Will I need an Executive Summary Presentation or just a short formatted bid sheet?

- Survey findings revealed the following risk exposure:
- List the current loss numbers – shrink%, claims costs, etc
- Potential loss exposure due to missing elements of protection are:
- Explanation of why recommended improvements are needed.
- Explaining the tie in of policies and procedures to manage the systems.
- How do you best explain the cost of equipment and installation?
- What about overcoming objections and the loss money on the table that pays for the program?
- What should be considered before agreeing on an implementation timetable?
- Should you be sensitive to install/service "blackout" times to minimize disruption?
- How do you go about closing the deal?
- Any final considerations to getting it in writing?

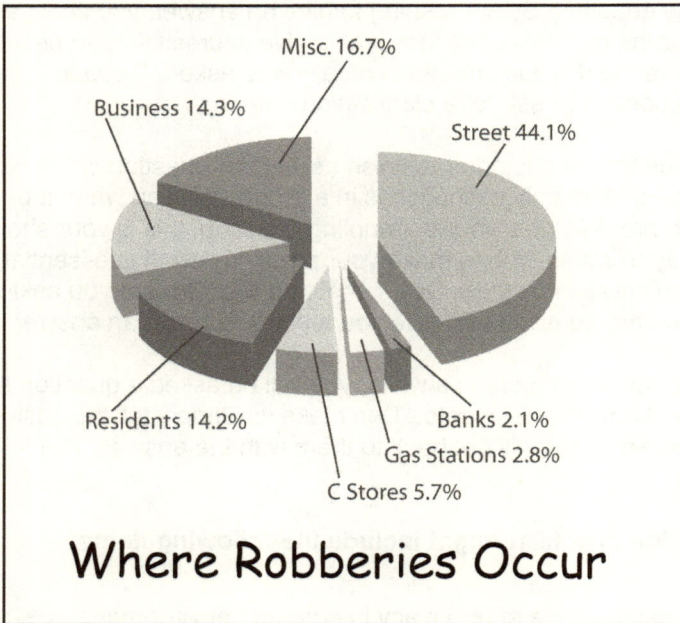

Misc. 16.7%
Business 14.3%
Street 44.1%
Residents 14.2%
Banks 2.1%
Gas Stations 2.8%
C Stores 5.7%

Where Robberies Occur

Teach your customers about
their crime exposure!

Daryl Closes the deal with the King Happy Food
Folks and AAA Security Team members
Amanda and Rodney arrive to start the job!

Big jobs need a lot of cable!

Chapter 8

Partnering With Professional Service Providers

AAA Security Team electrician and ladder pro
Mr. B arrives to start pulling cable and hanging
all of those cameras!

Mr. B is a sub-contractor that Daryl uses to insure
professional system connections and satisfies local
ordinances to use a licensed electrician.

**Chapter 8   Partnering With Subs and Professional
                 Service Providers**

We can best rename this chapter as identifying and working with skilled
professionals. But don't let the name scare you off. These are people that
should be looked upon as *sub-contractors* who can help you make more
money!

Let's describe a few examples of people you can use to enhance your
service offerings. Start with any activity or product that you want to make
available to your customers and decide through a skills analysis of your
business whether your or your employees are qualified to perform all of the
functions necessary to complete the project profitably. If you answered "no"
to a number of tasks that the project requires a reasonable level of competency, you can either choose to not pursue the project or you can partner or
sub-contract with another business to perform the elements of the job that
you either do not want to or cannot perform yourself.

We used an example earlier of an alarm-based business we know that
specifically advertised that they perform all sorts of electronic system installations and service except for mechanical lock work. Aside from the point
of pushing aside seemingly unwanted business and potentially losing the
opportunity to sell a conversion from mechanical locks to an electronic access control system, what's so hard about finding a good door guy to handle
that end of the business? The secret is finding a like-minded company that
is highly competent at door and mechanical hardware installation but has a
lower comfort level when it comes to pulling cable and installing electrical
hardware systems.

The sub-contractor skills list of trades that you can partner with are familiar.

- Carpenters
- Electricians
- Architects
- Draftsmen
- Mechanical systems engineers
- Fire system installers
- What about Engineers?
- How about architects?
- What about security consultants Board Certified in Security Management
  (CPPs)?

In a previous Security Wise Group® book (**Competitive Advantage-Fixing Small Business Security And Safety Problems)** that was directed at retail business end users, we tell our customers to get some "Expert" advice. We mean that they need to locate a Certified Protection Professional (CPP) who has been board certified by the American Society for Industrial Security (ASIS). This organization is over 50 years old and has been recognized as the leading creator of national standards related to loss prevention management and has created the CPP certification to recognize education and experience achievement for security professionals.

Staff loss prevention management in large companies are generally expected to have the CPP designation and provide the expertise that they need to reduce crime losses and claims. Most smaller companies probably need one too but cannot afford to have one of these people on their staff full time.

You can acquire the expertise of a CPP on an outsource basis when you need it, for as long as you need it. They are another sub-contractor that you can use to leverage your business comparative advantage.

Here's why.

The ASIS certification program is the first and only program of its kind to be awarded a coveted Designation by the U.S. Department of Homeland Security (DHS) under the **Support Anti-Terrorism by Fostering Effective Technology (SAFETY) Act of 2002.**

What is the SAFETY Act?

The purpose of the SAFETY Act is to ensure that the threat of liability does not deter manufacturers of anti-terrorism technologies from developing and commercializing new products that could significantly reduce the risks or effects of terrorist events. Companies that supply products and services that can be used to detect, defend against, or respond to acts of terrorism can apply for and receive coverage under the law.

Although this legislation was largely intended for product manufacturers, ASIS took the unprecedented step of convincing DHS that the legislation also should apply to non-traditional products and services, specifically ASIS guidelines and certification programs. This groundbreaking initiative on behalf of ASIS members and other security practitioners has had beneficial outcomes in both arenas, with guidelines receiving the SAFETY Act Designation in May 2005; certification in July 2006 after two years of effort.

What does this mean?

The SAFETY Act Designation gives ASIS board-certified professionals, their employers, and their customers immediate protection from lawsuits involving ASIS certification and the ASIS certification process that arise out of an act of terrorism. Not only does it limit the types of liability claims that can be brought against a certificant, but it also entitles the certificant to immediate dismissal of those specific types of claims. Employers of ASIS certified practitioners also gain protection against terror-related liability claims that can include a presumption of dismissal from a lawsuit.

What does this mean for employers of ASIS board-certified personnel?

In addition to the many benefits of having ASIS board-certified practitioners on staff, the scope of liability protection granted by DHS is a significant corporate benefit that can be used as an integral part of business strategy.

While the SAFETY Act will not prevent all terror-related claims against employers of personnel holding an ASIS certification, it should limit the types of claims that can be brought against them, thereby reducing the threat of onerous lawsuits.

The Certified Protection Professional educational program bestows these security experts with a significant ability to help those that employ them reduce liability exposure when defending against allegations of inadequate security in the context of premises liability litigation. While the act relates to acts of terrorism, it is clear that utilizing the certification defense as stated in the description of The SAFETY Act of 2002, will certainly extend to cases where criminal attacks have occurred on private property. A terror attack is, after all, simply another criminal act but with a supposed political motive!

In our opinion, this all means that if you have your customers company Loss Prevention Program designed by a Certified Protection Professional, they and you will be able to mitigate a lot of liability exposure against allegations of negligent security claims. At the least, your due diligence in employing expert advice will be difficult to dispute and you usually get sued for what the plaintiff says you did not do versus what you did in many of these third party liability cases.

The CPP loss prevention professional has the experience to help you to identify your best alternatives for addressing loss vulnerabilities and give you assistance in developing a time line priority plan to put the program into motion so you can co-ordinate the efforts of various providers.   Most importantly, your CPP has the expertise to help you to write and implement policies and procedures that your customers need to ensure the best use of your equipment and to hold their employees accountable for maintaining and supporting their company loss prevention efforts.

Your collaboration with a CPP loss prevention professional can contribute significantly to the assessment of your customers company operations and give you, on a fee for service basis, a major jump start by:

• Conducting a loss prevention survey observing the latest industry guidelines to identify missing, outdated or ineffective programs, policies and equipment.

• Presenting recommendations for the creation of policies and procedures and recommendations regarding security hardware that is needed (that you install).

• Helping you to create an implementation plan that you can use to introduce the needed components of a security system proposal using a cost effective and affordable time-line.

• Assisting you with the creation of the program written elements such as manuals and handbooks and assist you're people with implementation and training.

• Assist you or directly participate in the program rollout.

Expert advice should be part of every business toolbox. An opportunity also arises from relationships that have recurring income potential. Many professional consulting services will negotiate a recurring fee and/or return business agreements with your company, if you partner them with your end user companies. They may end up being a free sales force for you and your products and provide you with viral marketing to their customers that may need your services. Here are some additional thoughts:

• Should you hire a sales Pro? If you do not have someone who can proactively seek out your most profitable jobs, aren't you just in a reactive mode?

• How do you select alarm-monitoring companies? Every alarm job needs a contract to protect you. All alarm monitoring companies have them and you need it too! "The reason alarm companies have so few lawsuits against them is the contracts. Without the contracts alarm companies would be involved in every case where there was an alarm and the subscriber suffered a loss". Ken Kirschenbaum Esq. has standardised contracts for all states at www.alarmcontracts.com. Check out this great source!

• How do you use Business Development Experts? JoeyD will tell you that what he does best is to guide businesses through the process of planning for growth, creating and executing marketing strategies that work. You really just need to find the right marketing Outsource Pro to help you begin to transition to a proactive organization.

Daryl knows that expert
advice should be a part of every
business toolbox!

Daryl knows that after the plan is
created you just need to follow it!

Mr. B Knows that every job needs help!

Chapter 9   Event Oriented Marketing

Event marketing is less about direct sales and more about public relations and business recognition. A well thought out marketing plan will benefit from including activities that are merely designed to raise your businesses status in the local business-to-business market place. You might honestly call it a little shameless self-promotion! (see Chapter 16 for ours!)

It's about creating an opportunity that is to your benefit because it draws your customers in and allows you to spend quality time with them away from the distractions of their home turf. While this sort of activity will likely not close any business deals, it creates a contact basis to share mutual concerns, issues and interests in your local community that you can use as a platform for a follow-up conversation and even a proposal.

So what is it? It's a planned function that you invite the business community to participate in that the attendees have an expectation that they will be will have the opportunity to network, get some face time with their own customers and eat some free food that you provide.

Of course, you aren't going to call it "event marketing" when you invite the business community to your function. You would typically use a euphemism such as "Customer Appreciation Day Barbecue" or in the guise of an educational event involving a speaker, a book signing, a local government figure or celebrity. So you are expressing thanks for past business, announcing new programs, announcing new services and perhaps showcasing new technology that you sell, install and service. Presenting new information to benefit your customers.

For purposes of our discussion, we will assume that you have a modest marketing budget but would certainly like to maximize the results. Whether you have a fairly large budget or not, you need a plan! By "Plan" we mean that you need a written event script that will be used to diagram the event timeline.

An early part of the planning process should include some research into whether other businesses in your community have pulled off similar successful events in the past. Why were they successful? You can ask around and see if you can find any attendees who can tell you what they liked or did not like about the functions that they have attended in the past. Ask your customers what they want in a networking function that will get them to come.

Once you have decided on the type of event that you are comfortable with, you can start the creation of a time-line plan that includes all of the pre-event planning issues laid out on a two or three month calendar leading up to the big day. Based on the type of event be it outdoor or indoor, you should take a look a community calendars published by local business groups such as the Chamber Of Commerce to identify any conflicts with other events that are likely to draw your target audience.

Clearly, putting together a marketing event takes time. Think about it, and it is no different than planning any other social event. Think about what would have to be done if you were to put together a family reunion for instance.

You would probably make a list of all of the things that would need to be done to put the event in motion.

• Call family members and get feedback about the best time to have it to insure maximum attendance.
• What would invitations say and how far in advance do you need send them.
• Plan on making a budget and determining who will pay for what and get buy in.
• Put together a food menu and determine who will bring what items.
• And etcetera...

You get the idea. You make a long list of to-do's and sort them into a time line illustrating when each item needs to be completed.

If you find that there are a lot of similar activities going on when you want to conduct your event, should you explore the possibility of participating as a sponsor at a larger event? You may be surprised to find out how appreciated other event organizers are to learn that you would like to be responsible for part of their program. Nothing wrong with taking part of the credit for an overall successful event that benefits a number of other sponsors. That is as long as it does not include your competitors! Then again, if it is for a really good cause, it can't hurt. Can you piggy-back on other events? We think so.

Depending on the venue, you may want to include speakers, authors or experts that can be used as headliners for your event. You may be able to utilize a number of community resources to be a point of interest to the attendees. You can approach community crime prevention officers from the local police department, fire marshals or other officials from the fire department, the Mayor, state assemblyman or any number of other public functionaries who participate in outreach activities for the local business community or otherwise need your support and/or votes!

Authors of business books may well be available. If your field is security, authors of books on loss prevention may be of great interest for your customers to meet at a book-signing event. You can see more about this in our last chapter.

How you select an indoor event venue or environment is very important. You may find a low cost venue space can be provided by business or other organizations that you belong to, clubs or even distributors or perhaps even one of your customers.

The idea is to have enough room to run the function without crowding too much or being lost in a space that is too large. If you invite speakers or presenters, you will need to have the appropriate audiovisual equipment and power supply. Many presenters use Power Point or similar programs that require a laptop computer, projector and a screen.

Food service considerations should include refrigeration and sanitary food preparation areas or just have the event catered. Remember, your invitees just want to chat with one another and nibble on the free food.

Menu suggestions for indoor and outdoor functions consisting of foods that you have really liked that did not interfere with talking and weren't too messy should be a consideration.

Commercial meeting spaces can provide the environment your looking for and many restaurants have private side rooms that are also a possibility. If you are forced to negotiate with hotel, catering hall or restaurant meeting planners, be sure that all costs are covered in writing in your contract.

What governs the invitation process? Timing around seasons or other events that are occurring? Will you need to have RSVP on your invitations to determine head counts?

What are some AV equipment considerations? Will you need to have screens, projectors or large monitors to showcase your products?

Should you provide door prizes and free service incentives – everybody gets something? Can you get your suppliers and distributors to donate products for door prizes?

For a business-to-business event crowd, should you avoid other promotional media at the event and just stick with a business card bowl that you can also use to draw door prize winners from? Don't forget to have everyone put his or her E-mail address on his or her business card so you can follow up later. We are amazed that many business people still do not list their E-mail address on their cards!

What can you do to maximize your face time with your customers? To start with, you need to be available to work the room and you can't do that very well if you plant yourself behind the grill in a production line cooking hamburgers! Delegate that job.

What about golf or other sporting events? Many organizations we know simply cannot have an event unless it includes a golf outing. If that is your passion (and you know who you are!) this type of event can be a huge draw especially if it benefits a local charity or non-profit community service.

What conversational techniques will surface customer needs? What keeps you up at night? Did you hear about the burglary the other night? Did you see the crime rates just announced by the police chief?

What's the best way to make follow- up appointments? We have found that many times getting follow up appointments is like pulling teeth once you have lost the face to face opportunity of your event.

What about event frequency? How often you should hold your events depends on whether you plan on doing different presentations for different groups. The answer may be that it depends on what the response is from the attendees. A rave review and increased sales make a repeat event a no brainer in three to six months depending on how much lead time was required for the venue and other planning considerations!

Selecting your customers by invitee diversity can be another issue. Should you be aware of potential conflicts among invitees and just invite non-competitive invitees? Should you avoid the hostile glares? Well it's probably not a major concern unless a fight breaks out!

How do you budget for the event? To make sure that costs do not run away from the realistic amount that you want to spend, it's a good idea to create a budget and try to plan with in the amount. While there may still be surprises in store as you go, your first event should be kept simple and low cost unless you see a direct return on your investment like filling a good sized room with paying customers there to listen to an event speaker or some such.

How do you measure success?

We think that the answer to that question is a little hard to quantify. In general, you should experience an increase in sales or other tangible results if you have done your job and followed up on all of the leads you can from the event.

Post Event Follow-up

The parties over and you know find yourself in a position to figure out the "so what" part of the event. If you haven't already started to read through notes that you made during the event, you need to make a prioritized list of people that you need to contact as an event follow up. Call, thank them for coming and ask when it might be convenient to get together to further discuss business.

In general, what should you communicate with your customers about in a post-event call or message? It's a great idea to express "thanks for coming" or "sorry we did not get a chance to talk" or "sorry we missed you" if that's the case.   Preview of future events can be discussed and get feedback about whether they enjoyed attending your event and:

* What did you like and want more of?
* What would you like less of?
* Too long?
* Too short?
* Like or dislike about the venue?
* Time of day?
* Day of week?
* Food and hospitality critique?

Even if your first event is not what you expected, getting feedback and learning from your mistakes will make the next one easier! The idea is to not become gun-shy from your first experience.

Professional meeting planners know that the devil is in the details and every successful event is the result of a lot of planning and experience from the past when things went wrong!

Portland has 10 ways over the river to get to the city. Each route has it's positives and negatives depending what your goal is when you get there!

Your Roadmap Plan, that includes your sales initiatives, is a bridge that transitions your company to the next level!

An event is a bridge to your customers!

Chapter 10

Newsletters
And E-mail
Communication

Daryl has his newsletters
professionally created for him!

Chapter 10   Keep Your Customers Informed With Newsletters And E-mail Communication

How do you go about finding out customers preferred method of receiving information from you?

- What are considerations about E-mail verses Snail mail vs. Fax?
- What are some newsletter content sources you can use?
- How can you get help with product announcements?
- Where do you find industry news items your customers may like to hear about?

Joey D's Lessons Learned - Marketing that Does Not Work

There are 64,000 people in your mid-size city. You've been in the locksmith and security hardware business a long time. You are known throughout the community and have a moderately high profile as a quality service provider.

Over time, Home Depot & Lowe's have located in your town and they sell a lot of hardware but you are not really feeling negative about it. In fact you might be getting residual business with keying and installation services. Suddenly, you have real competition; a new security company has come to town. Actually what happened is a low-key local fellow got an investment partner and they have become affiliated with a "name" alarm company. They now have multiple "sales people" on the phones and on the road and you can feel a definite slowdown in your commercial work and suspect it in your residential business.

You get a brainstorm and decide to fight back! You buy a mailing list of all the businesses in town and make a pledge to let them all know you are the oldest game in town, and you want to tell your security story.

You buy that mailing list of the 2,000 legitimate businesses. You prepare a Company History with a couple of testimonials and a few product logos and do a one-time mailing. You wait one week, a few envelopes come back, moved no forwarding but no calls. You wait two weeks; a few more envelopes returned but still nothing, no calls. After three weeks, you are not feeling real good, you've got a pile of returned envelopes and you can't account for a single phone call or walk-in that you can absolutely tie to the mailing.

What went wrong? (Basically Everything....)

The average adult needs to hear something 5-7 times before it sinks in! In order to change a habit, a repetitive action takes 16 times for it to become "automatic". Advertising is something else again, what you need are the multiple impressions that are required.

Circuit City, Best Buy and Radio Shack among many others have inserts in the Sunday Paper pretty much 52 Sunday's a year. Are you buying from these places every day? Don't you see their signs at every mall you pass by? When you see Circuit City do you automatically think electronics? Effective advertising takes time to make an impression and even with that there is no guarantee!

Direct mail typically gets a 1-2% response, and not all respondents are buyers! So for a single mailing to 2,000 businesses, if you had a compelling offer you might be able to solicit 20 to 40 customers, and that's about it!

Most lists are not 100% accurate. Who moved, got transferred, changed phones, added new contacts, it seems most lists are about 80% accurate to start with. Then, you take out the repeats and suddenly the 2000 member list becomes 1700 and now you are looking at 17 to 34 responses being considered about right...discouraging?

The lesson, of course, is don't invest in a single one-shot mailing. You must commit to at least 4 times a year, 12 are better and every other week could be the most effective work. If you want direct mail to succeed, it has to be frequent. The message must contain a "take action" invitation, and a timed message can drive response to.

Direct Mail and Written Communication

E-mail: The Ideal Viral Marketing Tool

E-mail is an extremely fast and cost-effective viral marketing tool, especially for small business owners with little or no marketing budget. In today's wired world, an E-mail sent to a contact list of only 20 people could potentially end up in the inboxes of hundreds, thousands, or even millions of "friends" around the globe. When an E-mail campaign travels beyond its original contact list, as recipients forward it to their friends, who forward it to their friends, and so on, we refer to it as "viral E-mail marketing". E-mail forwarding can lead to all sorts of added business benefits, all at no extra cost to you, but the viral component of your E-mail campaign should ultimately support a higher-level objective. Here are some campaign objectives that can be supported by viral E-mail marketing:

• Increasing brand exposure: Sometimes all you want to do is get noticed, to start the lengthy process of getting your brand in front of as many people as possible. Encourage forwarding in your E-mail and help your brand go farther.

• Growing your opt-in list: Get your readers to forward your E-mail, and as long as it has a sign-up offer, you can encourage new sign-ups and even match those sign ups to the readers who did the original forwarding. See the next bullet for more on this.

• Designing loyalty programs: If you knew who was forwarding your E-mails the most, and that those forwards were turning into new subscribers or sales, wouldn't you want to thank that person and encourage them to keep it up? Viral E-mail tracking systems can help you acknowledge or reward those special people who help you grow your business.

• Driving website traffic: If more people get your E-mail, more people will see and click on the link that takes them to your website-where they can be exposed to product information, cross-selling, sign-up offers, etc. Forwarding can only help you, but if you don't ask, people often don't even think to pass it along. Remind them in every E-mail.

• Generating revenue, directly from the E-mail: If your E-mail contains a "buy now" button, you can directly correlate forwarding to revenues. The math is simple: the more your E-mail is forwarded, the more likely you are to increase revenues beyond the original list's potential.

How often you issue a newsletter is really up to you. Generally most of the time you want to be in your customers front brain lobe as often as possible without becoming too often and thus boring. Receiving your newsletter should be a welcomed event and not just another piece of mail that comes every month. We think the answer falls between how often you can consistently write and edit the letter on a regular basis and how often your customers tell you that they actually take the time to read it.

Nature of the content is also tricky because it is often the case that you are going to run out of fresh product information or other new developments that may be of interest to your readers.

Examples of content could include the obvious technical developments occurring in your customers business sector, new security products of interest to either commercial customers or homeowners. Don't forget to talk about important community events or crime trends that can effect your customers along with your solutions to the problem.

It's always a great idea to get a local official to write a guest article or better yet a regular column.

Mail lists and where to get them are up to you with the warning that buying many commercially available lists may not target the desired demographic and may have many "bounces" indicating inaccurate E-mail addresses. We think that the best way to start your list is by joining and using the member list of various civic organizations and use their list. Send a letter of introduction to the members about your newsletter and ask them to "opt in" to receiving it. Use enticements or incentives such as periodic coupons or prizes or some free ads in your letter to get them on board.

What is "Spamming" and why you should avoid it? Spamming is basically sending large amounts of ads to a list of people that have not opted in to your program. Everybody with E-mail or a postal mail box knows what it is. It consists of unwelcome ads, flyers or messages to buy some product or service that you have no interest in.

Your Newsletter: The Basics

When designing your newsletter always keep in mind the amount of time you can expect your reader to spend viewing your newsletter. Everyone today is information hungry, but always in a hurry. How you display your content within your newsletter can capitalize on this assumption.

What Information Should You Include in Your Newsletter?

Obviously this will depend on your business and the audience in which you are marketing, but here are three more recommendations to add to the others.

Announcements:

Include recent information about your company and/or products that impacts your readers. For instance, you can include a link to an upcoming tradeshow where your company will be exhibiting or perhaps a seminar that your company will be sponsoring.

Articles:

Include an article that relates to your products or services and helps your readers. It is also a great idea to develop a resource library that contains additional articles and provide a link for your readers so they can find more information on similar topics.

Case Study:

Provide an example of a client who has achieved great results while using your products or services. This will help build credibility with your readers. Again, provide a link where your readers can view additional case studies.

Those are three key items to include in your newsletter. If you include these you are keeping your readers up to date on recent information about your products or services, including an article providing value on topics affecting them and by providing a case study you are proving to your readers that others are achieving success by using your products or services.

Making Your Articles Easier To Digest

Think of how we read newspapers; the same holds true for how we read material on the web. We skim headlines looking for something that interests us and only then will we begin reading an article. We also stop to view photographs and any visual cues offering greater insight as to the information held within an article. We see far too many articles within newsletters that are very long (greater than 900 words). When writing your article try to keep it at 800 words or less and break each section into smaller, easy to read blocks with bold headlines over each section. This will encourage your reader to skim your article and stop at each section they find interesting. If you are finding it impossible to trim your article simply find a good point within 800 or fewer words and provide a link to a webpage that contains the article in its entirety. (To learn more Click here!)

Sharing Your Newsletter with Others

Always give your readers a reason and a means by which to share your newsletter with others. By providing valuable and relevant content to your subscribers they will be inclined to share this information with others by forwarding your newsletter. If you use E-mail-marketing software, it should provide a "Forward-to-a-Friend" feature that inserts a link within the footer of your message allowing your readers to easily forward your newsletter. The goal is to obviously reach out to as many as possible by providing valuable, relevant, timely content, and an easy way for your readers to share this information with others.

Some other thoughts related to newsletters.

Technically speaking, newsletters take a significant amount of time and technical expertise to produce. Professional spreads are mostly accomplished using software programs such as Adobe InDesign, Quark Express and a few others. These programs are difficult to learn and best left up to people who crank out newsletters and other publications for a living.

You can use Microsoft Office if you are satisfied with the quality but it will look like a publication without good layout and photo capabilities.

It should be noted that any attempt to have your newsletters professionally printed requires the abilities of high-end software to create the pages, allow high resolution photo layouts and be able to convert the newsletter to a PDF file or Quark Express document.

We talk to many people who love the idea of a newsletter but simply do not know how to create one or think they do but never get around to it! We can share with you that professionally produced newsletters are available commercially for a number of sources including the authors of this book at Security Wise Group LLC®.

Security Searchlight for commercial customers is a choice you have if you don't want to do it yourself!

Amanda, Hannibal and Rodney know that the best
customer relations are gained by doing the job
right the first time!

Do-overs and Re-do's are not in our vocabulary!

Chapter 11   Build Relationships That Last

We're sure that you are familiar with the adage about a bird in the hand being worth two in the bush. The old saying is especially appropriate when talking about customers. We constantly hear the following statement from marketing professionals with a lot of academic credentials and experience. "On average, finding a new customer costs five times as much as keeping an existing one". Some experts claim an even higher ratio.

There are plenty of reasons to start marketing to your existing customer base. We are reading a lot lately about CRM or Customer Retention Management reaching the point of having a lot of serious science applied to the concept of what motivates your customers to remain with you or to migrate to other more attractive service providers.

Some of the following information about relationship marketing was gleaned from the online encyclopedia Wikipedia that includes a number of sources, most of which we list for further reading. Where we are unable to discover the exact source, we note the presence of an anonymous source. The main thing we would like you to remember is that there is a serious body of work attributed to academics at major universities who can offer lots of reasons to take a long look at your business plan in order to incorporate some important ideas and plans that have made some practitioners of these ideas very rich! So even if you aren't going to write down these names for further reading, we invite you to listen to some of their pontifications that make sense in the real world.

Relationship Marketing is a form of marketing that evolved from direct response marketing in the 60's and emerged in the 80's, in which emphasis is placed on building longer term relationships with customers rather than on individual transactions. It involves understanding the customers' needs as they go through their life cycles. It emphasizes providing a range of products or services to existing customers as they need them.

An early participant in the relationship marketing field, Leonard Berry, observed: "What is surprising is that researchers and businessmen have concentrated far more on how to attract customers to products and services than on how to retain customers". The early research was done at Texas A&M (Berry, L. 1982) and at Emory University (Jag Sheth), both of whom were early users of the term "Relationship Marketing", and by marketing theorist Theodore Levitt at Harvard (Levitt, T. 1983) who broadened the scope of marketing beyond individual transactions.

Aside from the academic discourse, relationship marketing appears to have originated in industrial and business-to-business markets where long-term contracts have been quite common for many years. The academics re-examined these industrial marketing practices and applied them to marketing proper. According to Leonard Berry, relationship marketing can be applied: "when there are alternatives to choose from; when the customer makes the selection decision; and when there is an ongoing and periodic desire for the product or service".

Other academics used the term "Defensive Marketing" to describe attempts to reduce customer turnover and increase customer loyalty. This customer-retention approach was contrasted with "offensive marketing" which involved obtaining new customers and increasing customers' purchase frequency.

Defensive marketing focused on reducing or managing the dissatisfaction of your customers, while offensive marketing focused on "liberating" dissatisfied customers from your competition and generating new customers. There are two components to defensive marketing: increasing customer satisfaction and increasing switching barriers.

Traditional marketing appears to have originated in the 60's and 1970's as companies found it more difficult to sell consumer products. Its consumer market origins molded traditional marketing into a system suitable for selling relatively low-value products to masses of customers. Over the decades, attempts have been made to broaden the scope of marketing, relationship marketing being one of these attempts. Marketing has been greatly enriched by these contributions and we think that you can be too!

The practice of relationship marketing has been greatly improved by a variety of customer relationship management software programs that allow tracking and analyzing of each customer's preferences, activities, tastes, likes, dislikes, and complaints. This is a huge advantage tool in any company's marketing strategy regardless of size and certainly beats filling out 3x5 cards.

One example we found described an automobile manufacturer maintaining a database of when and how repeat customers buy their products, the options they choose, the way they finance the purchase etc. This puts them in a superior competitive position to custom target sales material. In return, the customer benefits from the company tracking service schedules and communicating directly on issues like product recalls.

At the core of relationship marketing is the notion of customer retention. According to our favorite source Wikipedia ; "Relationship marketing involves the creation of new and mutual value between a supplier and individual customer. Novelty and mutuality deepen, extend and prolong relationships, creating yet more opportunities for customer and supplier to benefit one another" (source unknown).

Studies in several industries have shown that the cost of retaining an existing customer is only about 10% of the cost of acquiring a new customer so it can often make economic sense to pay more attention to existing customers. Earlier we quoted the ratio as 5 to 1, but as you can see, the percentage varies among many academics. The emphasis consistently shows that the big payback lies in retention activities.

There is claim that a 5% improvement in customer retention can cause an increase in profitability of between 25 and 85 percent in terms of net value depending on the industry. Accordingly, the increased profitability associated with customer retention efforts occurs due to the following line of reasoning: The cost of acquisition occurs only at the beginning of a relationship, so the longer the relationship, the lower the amortized cost. Account maintenance costs decline as a percentage of total costs (or as a percentage of revenue).

• Long-term customers tend to be less inclined to switch, and also tend to be less price sensitive. This can result in stable unit sales volume and increases in dollar-sales volume.

• Long-term customers may initiate free word of mouth promotions and referrals.

• Long-term customers are more likely to purchase ancillary products and high margin supplemental products.

Customers that stay with you tend to be satisfied with the relationship and are less likely to switch to competitors, making it difficult for competitors to enter the market or gain market share.

Regular customers tend to be less expensive to service because they are familiar with the process, require less "education", and are consistent in their order placement.

Increased customer retention and loyalty makes the employees' jobs easier and more satisfying. In turn, happy employees feed back into better customer satisfaction in a continuous circle.

Relationship marketers speak of the "relationship ladder of customer loyalty". It groups types of customers according to their level of loyalty. The ladder's first rung consists of "prospects", that is, people that have not purchased yet but are likely to in the future. The successive rungs of "customer", "client", "supporter", "advocate", and "partner" follow this.

The relationship marketer's objective is to get as many customers high up the ladder as possible. This usually involves providing more personalized service and providing service quality that exceeds expectations at each step.

Customer retention efforts involve considerations such as "Customer Valuation" which describes how to value customers and categorize them according to their financial and strategic value so that companies can decide where to invest for deeper relationships and which relationships need to be served differently or even terminated.

Customer retention measurement calculates a company's "customer retention rate". This is simply the percentage of customers at the beginning of the year that are still customers by the end of the year. In accordance with this statistic, an increase in retention rate from 80% to 90% according to the experts is associated with a doubling of the average life of a customer relationship from 5 to 10 years. This ratio can be used to make comparisons between products, between market segments, and over time.

Determining reasons for defection looks for the root causes, not mere symptoms. This involves probing for details when talking to former customers. Other techniques include the analysis of customers' complaints and competitive benchmarking. Here, again, we need to look at what our competitors can do better than us.

Developing and implementing a corrective plan from reactive to proactive, could involve actions to improve employee practices, using benchmarking to determine best corrective practices such as retraining employees, visible endorsement of top management and adjustments to the company's reward and recognition systems. This is another way of saying that maintaining well trained, well-compensated employees can be the key to keeping your customers. J.W. Marriott Sr., the hotel company founder, once told us to "Take care of the employees, and they will take care of the customers".

A technique to calculate the value to a firm of a sustained customer relationship has been developed. This calculation is typically called customer lifetime value.

Retention strategies also build barriers to customer switching. This can be done by product bundling which combines several products or services into one "package" and offers them at a single price, cross selling of related products to current customers, cross promotions discounts or other promotional incentives to purchasers of related products and loyalty programs such as giving incentives for frequent purchases. The bundling strategy is important to the security industry since so many of our hardware elements are interactive and we can include policies and procedures that manage the interconnectivity of the various loss barriers.

If we educate our customers relative to the connectivity relationships, it makes the prospect of switching individual elements by a competitor more difficult. Conversely, your efforts to get prospective customers to switch to your security plan proposal can be enhanced by presenting integrated systems that work well together versus piecemeal replacement of non-related components.

Many relationship marketers use a team-based approach. The rationale is that the more points of contact between the organization and customer, the stronger will be the bond, and the more secure the relationship. If you are a small company without a formal marketing department, you can still participate in many of these strategies by establishing these programs and assigning sales people to perform the role. You can also out-source your marketing program to professionals in the same way you have professionals provide accounting and human resource functions.

Relationship Marketing is cross-functional marketing. It is organized around processes that involve all aspects of the organization. Another way to say this is that "customer service relationship marketing is a part of everyone's job description in the organization". In fact, some commentators prefer to call relationship marketing "Relationship Management". We all acknowledge that marketing and customer service as inseparable.

Internal Marketing, another term coined by the academics, is relationship marketing that stresses what can be referred to as using marketing techniques within the organization itself. The claim is that many of the traditional marketing concepts can be used to determine what the needs of your employees are.

According to this theory, every employee, team, or department in your company is simultaneously a supplier and a customer of services and products. An employee obtains a service at a point in the value chain and then provides a service to another employee further along the value chain. If internal marketing is effective, every employee will both provide and receive exceptional service from and to other employees. It also helps employees understand the significance of their roles and how their roles relate to others'. If implemented well, it can also encourage every employee to see the process in terms of the customer's perception of value added, and the organization's strategic mission. Further, it is claimed that an effective internal marketing program is a pre-requisite for effective external marketing efforts.

The preceding is just a fancy way of saying that your ability as a business owner to involve all of the employees in your organization as part of your marketing strategy is imperative. If everyone understands that his or her role in the organization includes a large responsibility for customer satisfaction delivery, you are moving in the direction that will likely be the most successful.

Some of the marketing approaches central to relationship marketing are described as "internal markets, supplier markets, recruitment markets, referral markets, influence markets, and customer markets".

Referral marketing is developing and implementing a marketing plan to stimulate referrals. Although it may take months before you see the effect of referral marketing, this is often the most effective part of an overall marketing plan and the best use of resources.

Marketing to suppliers is aimed at ensuring a long-term conflict-free relationship in which all parties understand each other's needs and exceed each other's expectations. Such a strategy can reduce costs and improve quality.

Influencer marketing is a form of marketing that has emerged from a variety of recent practices and studies, in which focus is placed on specific key individuals (or types of individual) rather than the target market as a whole. It identifies the individuals that have influence over potential buyers, and orientates marketing activities around these influencers. Influencers may be potential buyers themselves, or (in the case of business-to-business transactions) they may be third parties.

Virtually all products have a service component to them and this service component has been getting larger in recent decades. Often, we have all found that the selling and actual quality of our service supersedes the sale of the actual physical product. Many customers just want to know that what we sell them will work well and that we will insure that it continues to work well with a minimum of disruption.

There are many expert strategies for motivating your customers to keep them coming back. We have listed a few that we found that make the most sense at the end of this chapter.

Joey D's Lessons From Successes – Be Flexible and Build Relationships!

Ever heard this complaint? "This customer can not be sold, he won't budge on the price, now I have to discount and I'll lose money"! Forget About it (fugetaboutit!). How many times do you need to hear this to get your competitive juices flowing?

A security business owner I know had an opportunity to sell 14 high security key control cylinders and 2200 cut keys to a condominium association. The stumbling block was not the price of the cut key, which the business owner had "discounted", but the price of the cylinders and the security business owner would not budge. On principle, of course!

At the time, the going rate for a cut high security key was 10.00 each. Our security business owner gave the customer a 12.00 price and discounted it by 20% for a 9.60 NET price each. This really satisfied the buyer who had wanted to report to his Condo Board that he had successfully negotiated a "deal" thereby saving over 5K which was indeed what they were looking for…inflated price or not.

However, the security business owner would not budge on the 60.00 per cylinder price because of the "principle of the thing" and the buyer would not say yes without a concession (especially since he got one already!) and no one was making a sale or buying a much-needed solution.

After two weeks, my sales rep called and said this big job is not going to happen and he was dejected and asked for me to call the security business owner. So I made the call and in conversation with the security business owner, my approach was to point out the facts and I told him: "The fourteen cylinders will cost you about $30 each or $420. You will make a gross profit of about $420.00 if you hold your price but on the other hand you are passing the whole deal up on 2200 keys x $9.60 each. The blanks on the deal will cost you $2.25 each, for a gross profit of $7.35 each". This means you are giving up $16,170 in gross profit for the "principle of the thing."

Is this a lesson you can afford to win on principle?

The security business owner began to "waffle" and reconsider his position when analyzing the real impact of his decision. To close the sale and make him go over the edge, I offered, why don't you go over there and give him the cylinders for FREE and make your customer happy while filling up your pockets!

I said, remember when you were a kid and Coca Cola came in glass bottles and you bought them in a vending machine? Coca Cola often gave away the machine in order to sell the bottles of Coca Cola. Genius when you think about it. It sure kept the merchant from stocking Pepsi!

The impact of making this deal was the end-user condo association would buy additional keys and add cylinders for years to come. Sometimes we have an opportunity in our midst but we get blind sided by stubbornness. You are in business to make money but sometimes you have to give a little to get a lot! And that is the bottom line reason for building business relationships that last.

How you communicate with your customers isn't that important; what's important is that you do it! One company that we know had a slogan of "TTM" which merely meant, "talk to me". Staying in touch with E-mail, newsletters, mailings, or a web-log (.blog). These methods remind your clients and customers that you're around when they need you. You can even call them to let them know about a sale, a new service you are offering, congratulate them on a recent event or just to ask if there's anything else you can do for them.

If you want your company name to be the first thing people think of when they need your product or service, you need to build personal relationships with your customers. That's why it's helpful to call or send a card on special occasions --like a birthday, anniversary, or promotion.

Letting them know you appreciate them builds a personal link and can help keep clients loyal. Something simple like sending a $5 gift certificate to a coffee chain and saying "Have a drink on me" goes a long way in relationship building. You may consider thank you notes to be no-brainers, but you'd be surprised at how many entrepreneurs neglect to write them. Take the time to show your customers that you genuinely appreciate their business, and they'll remember your thoughtfulness.

Linking up your clients and referring them business is a powerful way to encourage loyalty. People never forget who linked them up and by helping them grow their business, they in turn might need your services and products more as well.

Regular face-to-face contact is critical. Get together over coffee or lunch regularly, and try to spend time in a non-sales capacity. Entertaining clients at home with a networking cocktail party, where you can introduce them to others who also might help their businesses, gives clients a sense of belonging to your business community. Don't forget to get involved in your local chamber of commerce or service club meetings as a great way to have a venue that invites conversations away from the pressure to sell someone a product.

Just as an unhappy customer can cause a lot of damage to your business reputation, good customer service keeps customers coming back and brings in new customers over the long term. Managing your reputation is a key consideration.

If an article is written about your business or you are quoted in the newspaper or a magazine, send copies to your existing customers and clients. This will keep you in mind, bolster their confidence in you, and encourage them to recommend you to others. There really is a good reason for a little self-promotion when the opportunity arises.

Ask your existing customers if there are ways you can improve your product or service. When you ask customers for feedback and take their concerns seriously, they feel a sense of ownership in what you're doing and thus become more loyal to your products and services. If you do lose a customer and you still feel comfortable discussing your relationship, ask them to tell you if there was any particular reason that they are now doing business with a competitor. Don't miss out on the opportunity to correct a misconception or add a new service item that can keep you from losing other customers.

You can't expect to reach out to someone once and have a customer for life; you need to reach out to them regularly. Like anything worthwhile, consistent follow-up requires a lot of effort, but over time you'll reap the benefits of a steady stream of repeat business and referrals. We think that planned activities in your business marketing plan that schedules when contact initiatives will occur can help you maintain the momentum that you need to keep you on your customer's minds.

It's important to demonstrate your commitment to your community. If a client has a particular charitable venture, consider contributing time, money, or goods to the cause. Less obvious, is the need for all of us to "give back" a little to either those less fortunate or to a civic group that is highly dependant on volunteers to succeed.

So what are some of the other things that you can do to keep your name on your customer's front burner?

Remind your customers by:

• Send newsletters or e-zines

- Send articles of interest (about their industry, hobbies, etc.)
- Send birthday card (and gift)
- Send anniversary card
- Refer them to a website of interest
- Suggest and introduce to people who can be helpful
- Give a referral
- Send survey or ask for feedback about your services
- Invite to lunch, breakfast, dinner or coffee
- Send postcards
- Send holiday greetings-especially unusual holidays
- Send a book or other gift
- Drop by with a give-away
- Send audiotape or CD
- Give tickets to events
- Send E-mail messages
- Phone to see how everything is going
- Send a testimonial
- Send book reviews of interest
- Invite them to be your guest at an event or meeting
- Send announcement of upcoming events
- Ask for advice/recommendations
- Invite to an open house or other client appreciation event
- Send a puzzle with a message
- Send video of a workshop with popcorn
- Send a holiday gift for every holiday (especially the more obscure ones)
- Send them a list of ideas that would help their business.

Part II

Implementing Change
& Deciding To Take Action

The correct change is also
good for your bottom line!

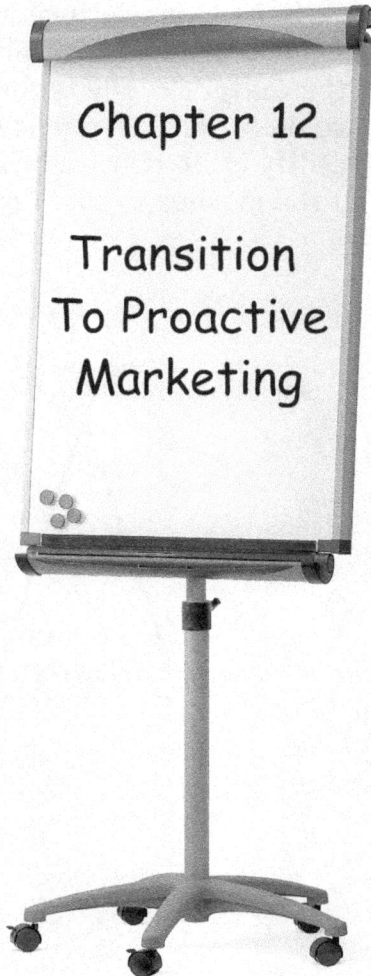

How to build a Successful Company

Central to the business is the COMPANY CULTURE, represented by a triangle, a symbol of strength. Consider your own company and the people in it with brutal honesty, does this triangle signify a strong culture from which you can build the business, or a weak culture where you are just surviving? Defining the Culture really is the responsibility of the owner. How we do it here....from how we personally look, how neat the facility is, to how we answer the phone to what we sell....it is all the makeup of the Company Culture!

The second piece of the successful company is the VISION. Without a vision you will not know where you are going or recognize it when you get there! The VISION is something to drive the company and its employees. Promoting the VISION is the responsibility of the business owner. You must have a vision for any size business whether a one-man band or one hundred employees. The risk is the VISION rests on the Company Culture and if the culture is weak the vision teeter totters and eventually backslides on the slippery slope of failure and the company never sustains growth.

This Vision thing is going to need a lotta Support!

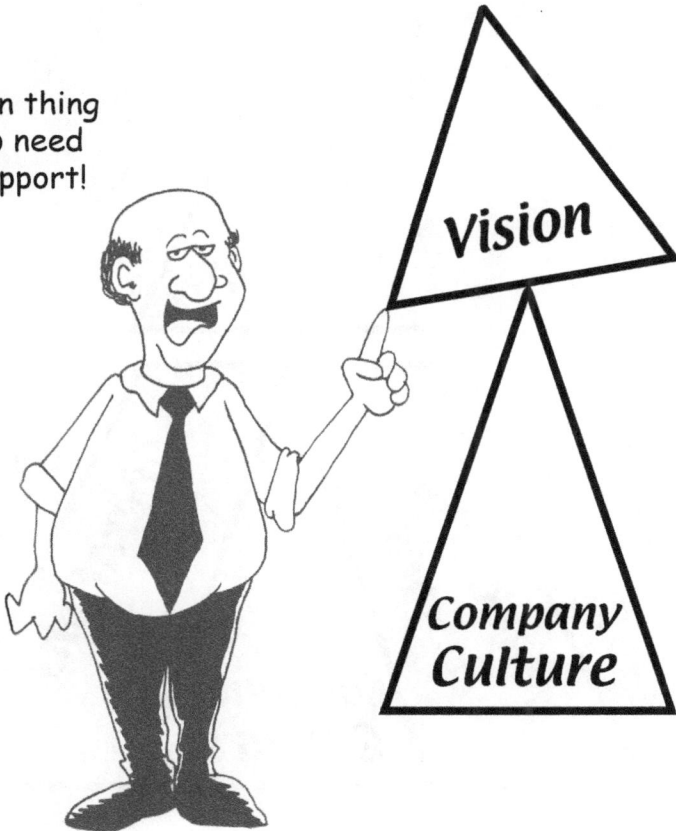

As the Owner, you can increase the likelihood of success by adding two pillars of strength to support the VISION Triangle, and with the addition of a Marketing and Sales Leg and an Operations Leg, we now have a larger triangle... supporting the culture. The significance of this is amazing when you consider you can not motivate people to greater productivity for the long term, but you can inspire people to achieve greater heights with policies, programs, procedures and processes to make them more productive. You owe it to the business and yourself to give it every chance to succeed!

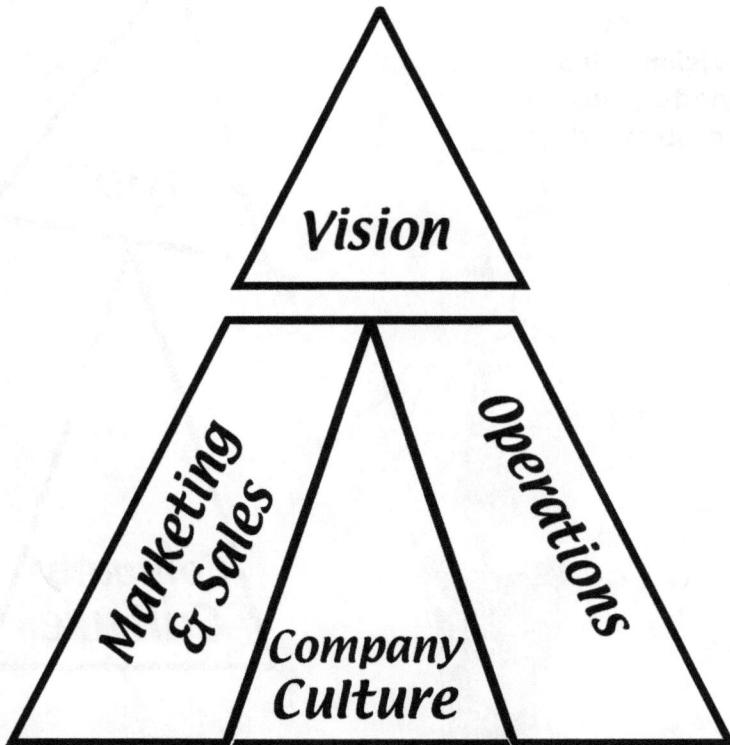

All of this is hype without the BASE of the Triangle, consisting of written Documentation and Training. If you want to succeed and make every employee as productive as possible, you must document every policy, procedure, and process and train consistently and constantly.

You now have all of the pieces to the puzzle!

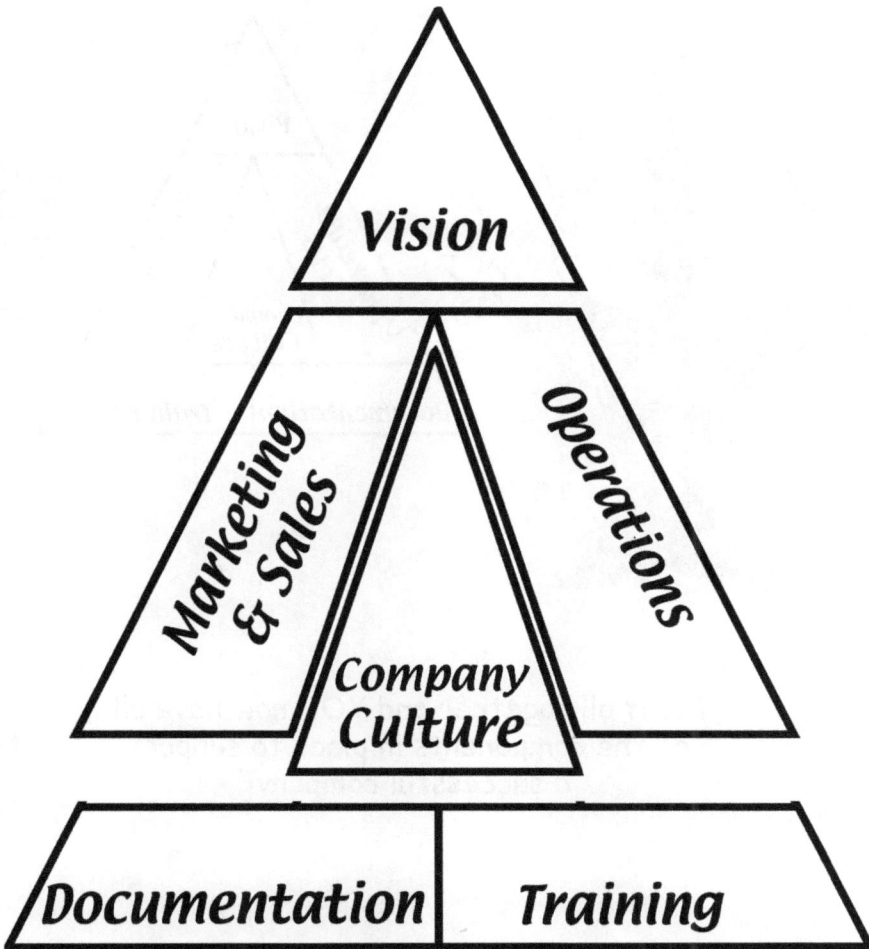

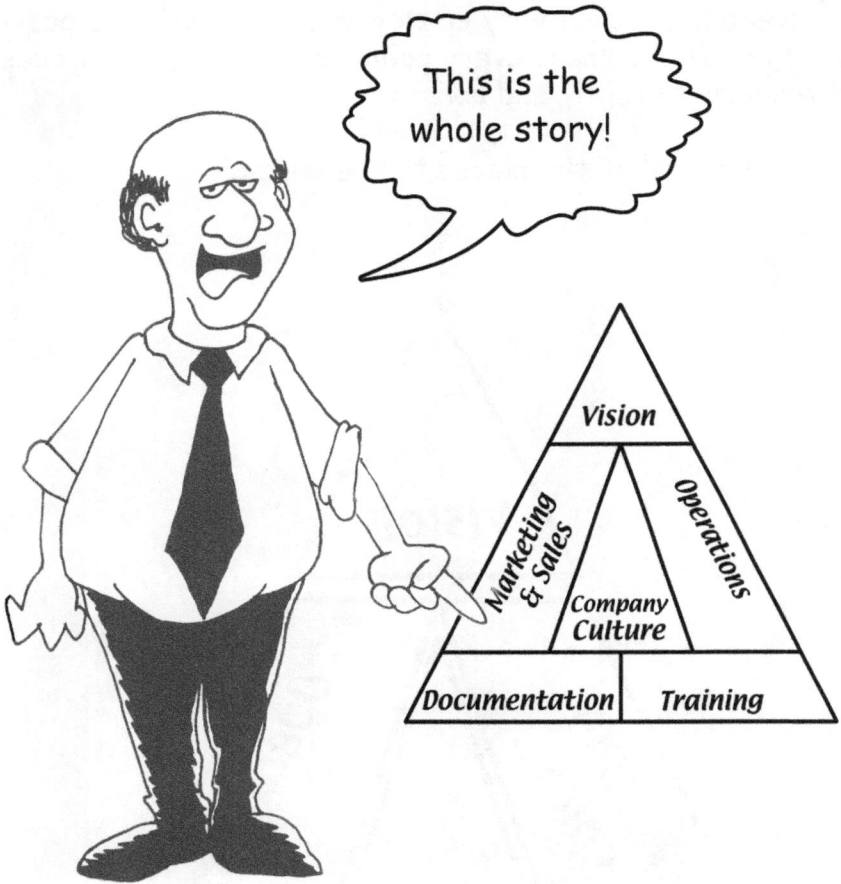

Put it all together and YOU now have all
of the components in place to support
a successful company!

Transition To Proactive Marketing

Those of you who have used this book as a learning roadmap, as we have intended it to be, have by now developed a pretty good idea about who they are in their marketplace and what direction they would like to see their business go. We must assume that the direction you have chosen will be to expand rather than contract your business venture. If you think about it, there are no other directions or options given the dynamics of the security products and services business segment. You really have to grow or experience being left in the dust by your competitors who have accelerated their business revenue by adopting a proactive marketing plan.

Assuming that sales orders from your most profitable demographic will continue to arrive from a yellow pages ad, should be recognized as not being a sustainable business model very quickly after your competitors target the same end users with aggressive marketing strategies that includes the creation of a professional sales and marketing department to drive their business. In fact, a progressive marketing plan may well eliminate the reactive yellow book advertising strategy all-together!

While business and economic trends are not absolute, they are nonetheless valuable to use when analyzing whether your own business tends to mirror the past and current market trends and future probabilities. In other words if your business is experiencing market demand changes such as the conversion of mechanical locking devices to electronic access control and you are not prepared to follow these trends, how long will it be before your resistance to change starts to be noticed as a revenue decline?

At this point for many security products businesses both locksmith based as well as alarm based, the adoption of systems integration approaches for your business development have proven to be the best direction for growth through the process of targeting the most profitable end users.

JoeyD's Lessons From Successes - Planning For Change!

Jim, a security business owner, was vexed, the locksmith business his Dad started forty years ago was now his baby and in five years he took it a long way from the repair shop of yesteryear to a security store of today. Jim grew up to be a terrific technician just like his Dad. When he took over the business he upgraded and up-dated the company image, acquired new capabilities, and was ready for the total security demands of his existing and many prospective customers.

Gone were the luggage lock repairs, bit and skeleton key locks, saw sharpening and door closer repair. In were CCTV, Electronic Access Control, Alarms, Key Systems and Systems Integrations capable of tying in with POS, HVAC, and Lighting. WOW, Jim was sitting alone one night after all the employees had left, looking around and thinking to himself, "We've transitioned and yet people just are not coming in like they used to when we were just a key shop, man did we have foot traffic then, and cash sales to boot. What am I doing wrong? The place looks great, my techs are good, what can I do to drive traffic and grow the business?"

Jim thought to himself, the result of years of being a certified master locksmith and fine technician in my Fathers business with the great reputation did not prepare me for this. He spoke to his wife for her thoughts. She said with all the time and money you have invested, and time away from the family, why not sell the business move to the coast and sell real estate? Jim knew he needed outside help!

Jim thought, "It is time for thinking out of the box." He wondered if perhaps talking to someone who went through a similar experience with a security background might be able to help. Although he was a member of the national and local trade organizations, there was no formal central point of contact to discuss business development, marketing and sales ideas. Plenty of technical training, but no business training! Jim thought, how ironic, with the skills to do the actual work, what a waste if you could not get enough work to make ends meet!

So, considering he needed to talk to someone. He opened his Rolodex, which was just half transferred to his computer, something more important always seemed to pop up, fumbling through the hard copy, he found the name of a fellow he knew from years ago that moved from the technician post in a family business through sales and sales management positions in manufacturing and distribution to a prominent business development position in the industry. This old acquaintance Gaetano DeAngelo was the guy to call!

Jim called Gaetano and after several minutes of friendly exchange catching up on old times, Jim told him he now owned the family business. He added that he spent most of his adult life as an eager technician and not a business generating rainmaker. He told Gaetano; "Competition is tough, and the customers are not calling us for big jobs, more of the small things and stuff others can not do." Business is not as automatic as it seemed in the old days. We need to change how we get business. Waiting for the phone to ring is not working for us."

Gaetano knew during Jim's years in the business there was little or no formal training on marketing and sales. Most marketing money was spent on truck painting and yellow page advertising and the sponsorship of a local Little League Team. Other money was spent on annual product training and that was about it.

Gaetano told Jim in the old days it was the guy across town your father worried about, today with the introduction of CCTV, Electronic Access Control and Alarm sales, the competitors are powerhouses and big names such as ADT, Honeywell, Brinks, Stanley, and many more. You have to take some drastic steps to move from "your Fathers lock shop" to a worthy competitor. You must have a marketing and operations plan and people capable of executing a sales plan.

Jim exclaimed, "We're not sales people." Gaetano said you could change! You were not born a technician either, but you learned along the way! Marketing and sales are skill sets, attitudes and processes and procedures you must execute. It really is no different than learning how to program a stand-alone access control product for the first time."

Gaetano then said, "Nothing happens until something is sold!" How many times have you heard that old adage Jim? If you are going to generate new business with existing customers and new business with prospects, you must proactively sell! Jim was getting excited! How do we begin selling?

Gaetano offered, "You must be proactive. You cannot afford to wait. Unlike the popular movie, A Field of Dreams, you can build it and they may never come! You have to reach out and touch someone! There are enough slogans to write a book, but isn't it the truth? Security is a high tech business but the customers are in a high touch mode. You must roll up your sleeves and dig into sales and marketing with the same zeal you attack new technology."

In order to compete today you must have a solid marketing plan based on facts. A solid plan is developed after a comprehensive analysis that truly defines the current reality.

Gaetano advised, a good analysis addresses the overall market and its' major segments. Today many end-users have Fire & Burglar Alarms that are sold separately from Closed Circuit Television and Electronic Access Controls, and mechanical hardware is typically provided by a separate entity as well. Jim thought, "Yeah, and my company seems to get the call after the fact."

Jim asked what was next and taking copious notes, Gaetano said, "It is important to identify the primary competitors and be sure to include local, regional or national companies." Gaetano then added, you should identify your present customer base and list what you are selling them. You can use a matrix that looks like a tick-tack-toe grid and list exclusive, mixed, exclusive to competitor across the top and along the side list annual sales dollars bottom left is under 25K, Middle is 26 to 50K and top left is 100K plus. Go through your customer list and fill out the grid for each of your top 50 or 100 customers. That will be a great exercise and reveal where we are.

Then identify all the companies and future prospects you want to target. Targeting is a science. You can start by identifying your most profitable product to your most profitable customers and then identify how many other companies are in the same business or with similar needs in the area in which you desire to do business.

As part of this preparation, you must list the products and services you sell or want to sell. You have primary products you promote, products you service and then things you do not do. It is important to identify as many as possible.

Start Date	Account/Prospect Name	Contact S/T/O	Urgency Hi/Lo	$ 1st PO	$ Year 1	$ Life	RFP Date	Present Date	RFQ Date	Quote Date	Next Step	Due Date!
					$	$	$						

This Form is NOT a CALL REPORT. It is a tracking tool to list and review incoming business. It is also a tool to assist in accurate forecast of all future business. Please list up to 25 of your hottest target projects.

FormTTF001110103

Definitions: Contact	NEXT STEP Examples:
S=Strategic decision maker, typically highest officials in company	a. Send Info b. Visit Site c. Submit Proposal
T=Tactical decision maker, typically "upper management" Director of Purchasing	d. New Contact e. Keying Conference
O=Operational Contact, typically the locksmith or carpenter shop at large end-users	f. Factory Training g. Joint Sales Call h. Company Tour

A comprehensive plan also includes current advertising & promotional efforts, whether simply yellow pages or cable and radio. You need to list everything you are doing so we can see a clear current reality in order to make a plan to your ultimate vision.

Your existing pricing philosophy is important, and it will also be important to understand the "market will bear" price too. The difference can make you a lot of money!

Based on future plans blended in with existing marketing efforts and there will likely be new things to do, perhaps eliminate others and blend other so this is a very important piece of the puzzle and should not be done last, you must prepare marketing financials, identifying cost, return on investment and a time line.

Gaetano said to help you get organized for this action plan, here is a project action plan form.

While it is quite important to get the analysis right, it is important that the content be accurate! You must have real goals internally but for external discussion should you need to visit the bank to fund some new ideas. Goals include: Understanding the Nature of the Market, Understanding Competitors and understanding this company.

The analysis will answer questions: How large is the Overall Market? Based on your existing business and targets? What is the growth rate of the market? If the segment you want to sell to is not growing, then there is a finite group of targets. This is not necessarily a bad thing, but you cannot plan and project to sell more than can be consumed within a given geography.

How is the Market Segmented? Is it really fire and burglar alarm companies selling just their specialty or they providing CCTV and Electronic Access Control as well, forgoing mechanical hardware? You will also identify any Current Trends and identify potential major shifts in the near future? With so much going on in the security channels, this will be very prudent to identify! What is the current condition of the Company compared to the segmented categories identified? Are you super strong in mechanical, and all other categories?

Does your current portfolio of products compete? Very important in the alarm and CCTV segments! Closer to home, what is the company share of the local or regional market you are doing business within? This will be an interesting measure.

One method is to define an area by geography, dividing your sales dollars into the population, i.e. 1,200,000 million people divided by 1,200,000 sales dollars equals one dollar per person. To project the sales dollars of your competitors into the population as a common denominator, use this "rule of thumb". Take the number of total employees times one hundred ten thousand dollars for ninety percent mechanical companies to get a reasonably accurate gross sales number.

Use two hundred twenty thousand per person for companies with a majority of business in the electronic security business. Based on those numbers, you can identify the share of the leading competitors. You may find in many markets there is not a single dominating force yet in others, a total dominator! Either way you can develop a winning strategy.

As a final piece of the analysis, you must identify which of the factors below drive the market. There are absolutes and variables in every market, but the better you complete this picture, the better the new plan will be. Is this market you are working in are the leading factors,

What About Specification:

Is IR, Assa Abloy, ADT, GE and others specifying you out? Are you in a price conscious market? Does advertising influence buying decisions? Is a knowledgeable focused on sales only force the key to success? Do innovative new products such as bump resistant locks and biometric access control turn your customers on? Is it a single source company with skill and product breadth and diversification?

When we complete the analysis, we can then plan a marketing and sales plan that can be executed!

Where Do You Start?

Joey D's Lessons Learned - An example of Highly Focused Marketing & Selling

A business owner of a larger security business requested some guidance from me in attracting new business. They had a great location, a superior list of repeat customers, great employees and plenty of desire to grow. The reactive business was steady, but how to get proactive and reach out to prospects was the real issue. So they sought my outside counsel.

So my questions began. I asked;" What is your most profitable sale?" The Owner thought about this and said, "Let me get back to you". He called a couple of days later and said, "We are selling a remote controlled electro-magnetic lock for public restrooms and we make a great buck on it." I asked; "How many have you sold and who is buying them?" The owner replied, "I'll get back to you."

Another day passed and he called to advise, "My people tell me privately owned stand-alone restaurants are buying these remote security devices due to a common problem in the downtown area, and apparently is expanding through the metro area phenomenon".

He continued his explanation by telling me that like many cities, there are many street people wandering around. There are common problems associated with "street people" including the usual "pan handling" that is bothersome, but imagine if these folks decided to use your restroom for the usual plus bathing and sleeping quarters! The police must be called on the trespassers and the response is typically long enough to potentially interrupt the normal balance of the restaurant, let alone make people uncomfortable throughout the process. And, of course, nobody can use the bathroom until these people are removed!

The security business owner added that the media has increased public and business awareness. There have been a number of television and news-print stories on this problem. People around town seem to recognize that the problem is growing.

This sounded like a great opportunity to proactively seek business with a known and effective solution. I asked how many they had already sold, the owner said, "We've sold about twelve of these…. (Nice!)" My next question to the owner was how many stand-alone independent restaurants there were in the metropolitan area, and the owner had no idea. We could have bought a list but in order to save time and money we looked in the local Yellow Pages and decided there were literally hundreds in the metropolitan area! A round number was agreed on, there were 600 potential clients!

It was agreed someone would copy all the restaurant names and local phone numbers.

Next we had to develop a script, a call plan and train someone to make the calls. Since his business was always very busy and making proactive calls would be tough to fit in, it was suggested a temporary person be hired. The temp. could work away form the hubbub of the busy location and move through the list. In fact, it would be better if the person had minimal knowl-edge and could not be tempted to talk too much or wander off the script.

A script was developed, a person hired and trained and the calling began. Contact was made with about half of the restaurants in the first week. The dialog went something like, "Good Morning are you the owner of the restau-rant? " Over half, or about 160 of those called, said "yes". Next they were asked; "Are you aware of the problem with street people entering the restau-rant to use the rest rooms and making a nuisance of themselves?"

Over two thirds, or about 110, acknowledged that they were experiencing the problem. The next question was: "Have you done anything to address the problem in your business? Nearly all said "no". They were then asked;

"would you like a proposal on a solution?", and 54% or 81 said YES! Eighteen of those asked for a quote and three of them ordered the solution sight unseen!

Sounds good doesn't it? Makes sense? Unfortunately, there is a flip side to the story related to execution and it explains why sales, marketing, purchasing, operations, installers, and basically the entire organization must be in tune for the marketing program to succeed. The first 3 installations were no problem. They were scheduled as regular work, materials were available locally and no issues arose.

But, for the people that wanted a proposal, there surfaced the question of "what to send them?" The owner said he had it covered but he found in the final analysis that a custom cover letter times the number of interested parties was too large of a job for the one in-house clerical support person to handle. On top of that there was not sufficient quantities available of appropriate collateral literature, a diagram or even instructions on how the system was supposed work, so the opportunity stalled!

The net result was over 150 people were interested, and very few were actually followed up with because they did not have the right collateral or sales person to go close the deal. Instead the opportunity spiraled downward to busy techs who were asked to "stop by when they had a chance". The chance, of course, did not come as everyone was too busy doing their ordinary work and techs are paid to install. Any time not installing cost the techs money according to the company compensation plan so the leads went cold and another well intended marketing and sales opportunity disappeared.

Failed marketing lessons can make you gun shy for a long time! The real lesson is that you must be prepared from beginning of a marketing project to end. As Steven Covey said in his The Seven Habits Of Highly Effective People, you should "see the end before you begin". A marketing and sales project without an operational plan, written documentation and training for all critical points and people is doomed to fail. In an unprepared "marketing plan" if you have any success at all it is more luck than anything and that is no way to build consistent success.

The Marketing Action Plan Should List A Set of Goals And Plan Actions Or Tasks To Be Performed To Complete The Goal

Strategy - Doing the RIGHT things
Tactics - Doing things RIGHT
Operations – Execution of the PLAN

OBJECT: Sell Hi-Security

Your belief and excitement might provide enough motivation for you to hope to succeed, but hope is not a strategy! For consistency and the long term, in effect repeatable business practices, you will achieve greater results by planning to win.

Developing a PLAN for Making Something Happen:

THE WHY

Our Security Solution is a method that enables you to pursue the goal with very little risk. For example, a plan goal statement might be: "Patented Key Control provides a value added attribute to all business and residential consumers. Preventing Unauthorized Key Duplication is something everyone recognizes as a method to increased security".

In this case your focus is affordable patented key control for the express purpose of preventing unauthorized key duplication.

Prepare a script for a short phone call where the ONLY goal is to agree on a time for a MEETING. Do not try to sell over the phone.

Example: "Hello Jim, this is Joe from Super Duper Security, we have provided you general lock service for years. We have something new I believe you will be interested in. Do you have twenty minutes "anytime soon?" Be more specific if your schedule allows such as, "Will Tuesday Morning or Wednesday Afternoon be better for you? Avoid "Yes or No" questions!

1.   Review your Customer List and identify who is not on a patented key control key system. This may be difficult if you do not have good record keeping, so in that case assume there is not a system in place.

2.   Make a List of Area Businesses that you would like to do business with. You have a legitimate story to tell!

3.   The tactics you will use are:

A.   Initiate Awareness via the Lock & Key System Analysis
B.   ID Recommended Lock & Key System Components
C.   Review key control management forms
D.   If the solution is agreeable, do Product Demonstration
E.   If approved, execute "count" and live Premise Survey
F.   Supply Written Quote with support collateral

Tracking the Operation via the SUCCESS TRACK

1.   Date: Target List
2.   Date: Qualified List
3.   Date: Recommendation Proposal/Presentation
4.   Date: Quote
5.   Date: Purchase Order
6.   How many at each Step?
7.   Are you moving the targets along?
8.   Are you on track, ahead or behind?
9.   Are there stalls at any one step?
10.   Meet with your Rep to review progress and Partner to break
        the barriers

Other Pro-Active Options to Consider:

1. Event Driven Marketing-invite business owners to enjoy light refreshments for a brief seminar on discouraging internal thievery and preventing loss in their business using patented key control-bring in a guest speaker to make it very special.

2. CO-Sales Visits to qualified end-users with Rep or Factory Executives, Director of Business Development or even the VP of Global Sales if the target is large enough.

- List of target customers
- Rethinking the marketing budget
- Developing the long term marketing plan
- One mailing per quarter
- One event 2-4 times a year
- Sales and marketing staff considerations
- Schedule a marketing event

Your event can be just having a few customers over for cocktails!

If you have been following along with our recommendations to create a Roadmap Plan by now you pretty much know where you are at from a marketplace position standpoint, you have performed a SWOT analysis and you have been looking at your company culture and assets and have begun to develop a vision of where you want to go in terms of business growth.

The real call to action is to sit down with all of the key people in your organization and agree on the plan content, who will be responsible for the plan initiatives and when it will be completed.

If you have not taken the time to create an organizational chart and a business function chart that aligns tasks under the direction of your key people, you have some remedial work to do before you create the content of your business plan!

Our illustration shows a typical business organization chart of the primary roles of Operations, Finance and Marketing. In a mid-sized company, these positions can have a number of different titles such as "Director of" or Manager" or might even simply be business partners who have agreed on what the division of labor will be in the organization. The assumption here is that the boss is really responsible for the results of the entire enterprise or at least a subdivision in the case of a larger organization.

Before you can logically create written job descriptions or agreements at

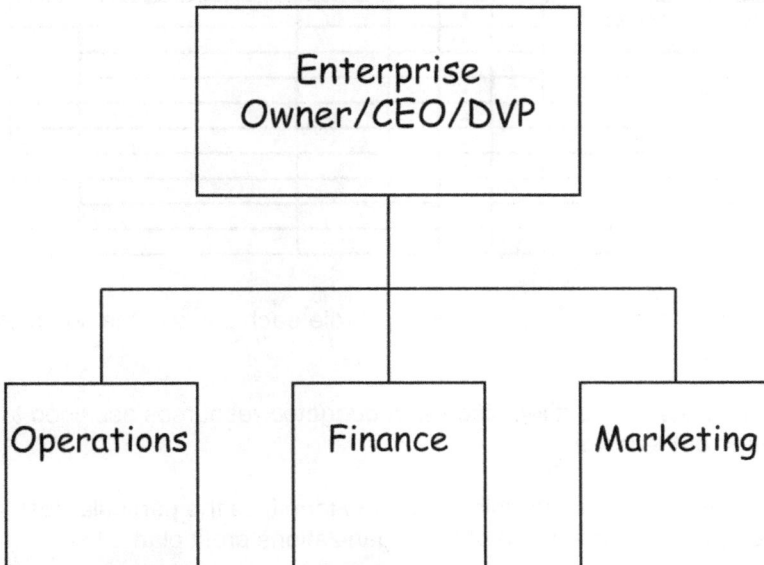

any level of the organization, it is important to identify all of the functional tasks that you perform within your company. A number of tasks my cross functional lines and as a rule decisions must be made related to who will be accountable.

As an example of this process, we can offer the following three charts that are really one continuous one that divides up tasks. Our example begins with what functions fall into the Operations realm delineating all of this particular organizations measurable tasks.

Operations positions needed to perform all of these functions will vary by organization, but will typically include all of the front line employees engaged in production, customer contact or clerks, line supervisors and the array of managers who are accountable for the performance of their subordinates.

Everyone all the way down the line from top to bottom needs to have a

Functions To Operate The Business (1)

FUNCTION	MKT	OPS	FIN	Position	Person	Date
Answer the Telephone		x				
Customer Service		x				
Dispatch		x				
Field Service-Architecture Hdwe		x				
Field Service-Auto		x				
Field Service-EAC,CCTV		x				
Field Service-Key Systems		x				
Field Service-Safes		x				
Field SURVEY		x				
Fleet Management		x				
Purchase		x				
Maintenance		x				
Set Up		x				
Hiring/Training		x				
Job Prep		x				
Job Scheduling		x				

written job description that identifies what role each plays in the completion of the tasks.

Marketing tasks are next identified with budgeted resources assigned to the completion of the tasks.

Finance is addressed in the third chart and identifies the particular tasks that the group performs in support of the organizations profit plan.

Functions To Operate The Business (2)

FUNCTION	MKT	OPS	FIN	Position	Person	Date
Keying Systems Preparation		x				
Lock Services-Bench		x				
Materials Handling		x				
Pick, Pack & Ship		x				
Technical Services		x				
Advertising	x					
Correspondence	x					
Field Sales	x					
Local Sales	x					
Regional Sales	x					
Field Service-Residential	x					
Marketing	x					
Concept/Implementation	x					
Fulfillment	x					
Phone Sales (Proactive)	x					

With the need to have job agreements/descriptions for every one of your employees is a very complicated process best achieved in larger organizations by your in house or outsourced Human Resources staff. Each position has to be analyzed with a formula such as sales per man hour or other measurements of return on investment.

Functions To Operate The Business (3)

FUNCTION	MKT	OPS	FIN	Position	Person	Date
Promotions	x					
Prepare Proposal	x					
Store Sales	x					
Accounts Payable			x			
Accounts Receivable			x			
Benefits Purchase & Admin			x			
Bookkeeping			x			
Computers & Equipment			x			
Human Resources			x			
Insurances			x			
Inventory			x			
Legal			x			
Payroll			x			
Purchasing-NEW			x			
Purchasing-Rebuy			x			
Prepare Quote			x			
Pricing			x			
Approve Credit			x			
Tax			x			
Workman's Comp			x			

Smaller organizations will find that many tasks that are occurring will not be delegated to subordinates because there may not be an actual person to delegate the task to. That means the person responsible for the function has to do it themselves or create a case to add an employee position.

Until you have identified what current employee position in your organization is charged with the responsibility for each functional task list, it is really difficult to create action plans that identify measurable tasks that must be performed in order to meet the goals of the business initiatives that you are trying to achieve. So again, like Steven Covey tells us in his 7 Habits Of Highly Effective People, "First Things First". By identifying the positional skills that exist in your organization you will know how much of a stretch it will be to change course and begin your transition to proactive marketing and sales.

A major piece of your planning process involves the format of the plan itself. It really is important to use tools that everyone understands to create a plan with a distinct process that will allow you to walk your key managers through a process that can then be used subsequently with their subordinates.

The planning format that we like and have used for a number of years is called "SMART Planning". We're not sure where this tool came from so credit will not be given. Coming from the corporate world, we have used it as an operational tool for at least 20 years.

The process takes off when a goal is determined by you and the key members of your organization. For instance, let's say that you are willing to use your people and resources to begin to transition into a more proactive business model by expanding sales into new electronic product installation and sales. The product selection needs to be made, you have to develop a budget to track the cost of sales and determine what an acceptable profit margin will be in both the short term and long term.

So you have researched a number of possibilities and have narrowed the selection to a particular manufacturer and model of an IP camera and recording system. You now need to put the process in writing!

So, what is SMART Planning?

The SMART acronym is used in your plan development as a tool to devise a system that you follow through to the completion of the goal! All of your goals are stated in terms of the five steps as you develop your plan

As it clearly states in this process, you have to be able to identify your specific goal or objective. The goal has to have measurable benefits to your company and action steps need to be identified to make the goal achievable and measurable. Resources to complete the goal must be identified such

SMART planning
What does it stand for?

Specific

SMART is an acronym that highlights the key requirements for any desired goal.

Measurable

Actions

Resources

Time

as sales program development, staffing to conduct the sales process and to fulfill orders. Often this is the hardest part of the process as it is likely that your resources have a limit and may seem to be already stretched. It's time to think about letting go of activities that are less profitable and consume more resources than they should.

SMART planning
What does it mean?

what are your **S**pecific objectives?

are there any **M**easurable benefits?

what **A**ctions need to be taken?

what **R**esources are required to achieve this?

how much **T**ime is required?

Finally, all of the actions steps must be time bound with measurable completed action steps by the end of your business year or whatever timeline you have decided is realist and achievable. The rest of the process is to decide who will be responsible for the completion of all of the action steps that you will identify as needed to complete the goal successfully.

The plan is completed on worksheets similar to the following example.

Use this form to complete all of your goals that need to be developed into action oriented steps that identify the completion dates for each and who will be responsible and accountable for the completion of the tasks.

This process will be pretty easy to put together if you have completed your business functions form that we showed you earlier in this chapter. Each of your goals will very likely involve operations, finance and marketing to a varying degree and you will need to determine where the resources will be coming from in order to support your goals.

SMART Plan - *(title here.)*

Target: *(Write the target of this document here)*   Department:

Specific	Measurable	Actions	Resources	Time
What specific objectives will achieve your target?	What are the measurable results of achieving your target?	What actions need to be compiled before your target can be achieved?	What resources do you require to complete each of the objectives?	What time is needed to complete each of the actions?

The SMART Plan form works as your template for all of the subordinate tasks that need to be developed and assigned to particular individuals or groups in support of your specific plan goals.

For instance, AAA security Service wants to expand their product and services offerings to include electronic access control as well as their Patented Key systems they currently sell. The stated goal is that a 10% increase in sales will occur as a result of changing emphasis away from work on key cutting and emergency lock out services which are low profit and high labor activities. To this end, AAA owner Daryl has decided to create a new work

group which will be called Corporate Accounts Group or CAG.
The planning process needed to be able to create the group and measure

AAA Security Solutions
Corporate Accounts Group
Sales and Marketing Plan
Measurable Objectives:
1. Grow sales with existing customers by 10% with sales support programs.
2. Presentation CAG to customers outlining strategies and anticipated results.
3. Increase sales by 5% identifying new sales alliance partnerships.
4. Assign roles and procedures within AAA To maximize results.

Goal #1 Grow sales by 10%

Create a unique sales and service support program for existing customers.

TACTICS	ACTIVITY	PLANNED DATE	PERSON RESPONSIBLE	ANTICIPATED IMPACT
Identify key elements that will be compelling, cost effective and create value added support for increased sales	Bullet point benefits to AAA and customers. Identify roles, resources and ROI	No later than W/E 11/01/08	Joey D (Director of Sales Mkt.) and Bill Wise CPP (Operations)	Create a desire to participate in the program developing increased sales opportunities through the dealer companies.
	Expand each point with explanatory information and illustrations	No later than W/E 11/01/08	MKT. and OPS. MKT. and OPS.	Develop understanding of use of CAG resources to increase sales opportunities.
Using written text and illustrations, show the benefits of alliance with CAG	Review and finalize presentation	No later than W/E 11/15/08		Insure a clear compelling reason to adopt CAG Strategy
	Publish completed Presentation Introduction to AAA	No later than 11/30/08	OPS.	Provide a consistent marketing approach to dealer partners

progress and success might at least partially look like the following plans.
Goal #1 is listed at the top of the page. The plan Tactics and activities are
listed as well as the time line/deadline for completion of each of the action
items. The Person responsible for the tasks completion is listed and the
anticipated impact is also described.

The next Goal can be detailed in the next planner form that is completed.
The purpose of this goal is to introduce to existing customers the new products and services that are to offered and will require further development
and planning of specific product offerings as well as the development of
sales collateral, product pricing, labor requirements that are anticipated and
overall detail development for the program implementation.

These tasks will be subordinate detail task planning in support of the overall
goal. So by stating the overall goal, the door opens to an extensive research and development initiative that must be identified and budgeted with
sufficient resources to support the successful program implementation.

It should be noted the research and development tasks that will be developed subsequently may impact the overall goal deadlines so care should be
taken to consult extensively with all of the people involved to make sure that

AAA Security Solutions
Corporate Accounts Group
Sales and Marketing Plan
Measurable Objectives:
1. Grow sales with existing customers by 10% with sales support programs.
2. Presentation CAG to customers outlining strategies and anticipated results.
3. Increase sales by 5% identifying new sales alliance partnerships.
4. Assign roles and procedures within AAA To maximize results.

Goal #2 Presentation of CAG support concept to customers

Create a Clear Written and illustrated Presentation to Motivate Customer Participation

TACTICS	ACTIVITY	PLANNED DATE	PERSON RESPONSIBLE	ANTICIPATED IMPACT
Present the benefits of CAG alliance to customers and end users using written storyboards. and illustrations	List a series of introduction statements. Explain why AAA distribution has created a CAG division to improve the depth of available customer services. Explain the experience and expertise behind CAG. Explain what they do and how they arrive at money saving strategies and recommendations. Create a descriptive statement for each illustration and a list of 4-5 talking points to describe what the	Beginning 12/1/08	CAG Sales & Service	Create interest in recovering end user profit through an alliance with AAA , CAG and adoption of LP strategies to create new sales opportunities for the customers. Instill a reason to trust the lengthy experience and well tested strategies of CAG and the AAA dealer to help prevent losses in the End User enterprise Sell the customer the interconnection of LP strategies and the result on their bottom
	illustration depicts. Identify "close the sale" strategies and scripts for customers.	Beginning 12/1/08	CAG Sales & Service	line profits. Obtain buy in and commitment

the due dates are realistic! The 3rd Goal involves using the new CAG group to increase existing sales by an additional 5% The purpose, of course, is to maximize the efficiency of the marketing group by extending a set of tasks of bringing in new customers at a sustainable rate that operations will be able

AAA Security Solutions
Corporate Accounts Group
Sales and Marketing Plan
Measurable Objectives:
1. Grow sales with existing customers by 10% with sales support programs.
2. Presentation CAG to customers outlining strategies and anticipated results.
3. Increase sales by 5% identifying new sales alliance partnerships.
4. Assign roles and procedures within AAA To maximize results.

Goal #3 Increase sales by 5% by identifying new customers

Create expanded sales by marketing the value of the AAA service program to new customers.

TACTICS	ACTIVITY	PLANNED DATE	PERSON RESPONSIBLE	ANTICIPATED IMPACT
Identify potential new customers using Sales Genie tools and business. contacts list Present unique value of the AAA CAG program	Identify potential East Coast customers. Initiate contact through Brochures, cut sheet. phone and post cards. Follow up with business. owners and supply catalog/web access. Provide training as needed for new	01/15/AAA Security Solutions	CAG Sales and Support	Increase AAA sales in a measured and sustainable manner by recruiting new customers through out the Eastern seaboard and other identified markets.
that adds new sales opportunities to their business.	dealer participation. Identify end users and maximize sales opportunities.			

to support.

The next Goal #4 represents an internal organizational change that needs to be made to identify all of the functions and tasks that take place on a daily, weekly or monthly basis in order to determine the organizations capability to

AAA Security Solutions
Corporate Accounts Group
Sales and Marketing Plan
Measurable Objectives:
1. Grow sales with existing customers by 10% with sales support programs.
2. Presentation CAG to customers outlining strategies and anticipated results.
3. Increase sales by 5% identifying new sales alliance partnerships.
4. Assign roles and procedures within AAA To maximize results.

Goal #4 Identify and Assign internal AAA /CAG organizational roles

Identify who will assume the job functions in support of AAA /CAG objectives.

TACTICS	ACTIVITY	PLANNED DATE	PERSON RESPONSIBLE	ANTICIPATED IMPACT
Define the core partner relationships within the AAA /CAG organization	Within the positions of Distributor, Dir. Of Sales, CPP Consulting, distribution center facilities, list all associated roles and activities. Define the scope of each role. Obtain commitment regarding the	W/E 11/1/08	Mkt. & Ops.	Insure business. and growth continuation through the adoption of defined roles and accountabilities within the organization. Set expectations for the position and the completion of
	execution and timelines. of task completion and resource availability.			tasks and goals. Measure success. through the completion of action plans and goals.

expand. As stated earlier in this chapter, it is likely that in order for the company to transform from a reactive mode to a proactive, changes in product and service must be considered. The low return high labor cost tasks need to be placed on a back burner and pursued as time allows with emphasis on doing what is the most profitable.

Needless to say, a great deal of work is needed to determine all of the subordinate tasks that must taken into consideration and then organized into a realistic achievable time line. The process works and is a great opportunity for the business owner to create a participative strategic planning process that will be needed going forward as the business works toward transitioning to proactive marketing and sales.

How detailed your SMART Plan should be is up to you. If the goal is complex, the plan will also need to have sufficient detail to perform all of the tasks needed to make it happen.

The more time you spend planning on the front end, the easier the execution!

> **Your NEW Paradigm**
> Your customer calls you, his Loss Prevention Expert, to solve a problem that he is having with excess inventory shrinkage due to an unknown reason. You have the systems, resources and expertise available to you to solve the customers' issue.
>
> Your new marketplace role is the winner!

Daryl's still looking for the
smartest way to do business!

**Chapter 13   The Selection, Care and Feeding of your Sales and
                  Marketing Department**

Jim and Gaetano decided it was time to have a person focused on marketing and sales to help the business grow. He thought long about the attributes, character and persona of the person he wanted to represent his best
interests in the field, someone who would buy into his vision for the future of
the company and would demonstrate fiduciary responsibility on the way to
generating business for the company.

In lieu of a sales job description which Gaetano saw as limiting, confining
and too much of a box from which to operate, he decided a position agreement was more suitable to the business and would mean more to each party
as time went on.

Instead of calling this position a sales position with a sales title, and potentially scaring prospects and customers with the dreaded "sales-guy or sales
gal" name tag, Gaetano opted for the title of Business Generation Representative for any person holding a field sales position at the Company. He did
give thought to keeping sales in the title so prospects and customers would
know by the name, the nature of the business to be conducted, but after
careful considerations and internal debate, opted for the softer title.

Gaetano thought further, the "position agreement" had to be written. He got
out a yellow lined paper (old fashioned as it may seem) some post-it note
pads and got to work by placing random thoughts on the post-its (limiting
himself to a few words per note page, then arranged them in a sensible
order)

He summarized:

- The Business Generation Manager Position is a proactive business
  position in this business and;

- Persons in this position are responsible for consistent, accurate and
  timely execution of all marketing programs and sales processes and
  procedures.

- Persons in this position are held accountable for results by the Business
  Owner or person appointed by the Business Owner to a Business
  management position.

- Persons in this position are expected to work within the paper and
  electronic operating systems of the Company.

- Persons in this business generation position are expected to be in the field 60% of the work week, with 40% for preparation, communications and follow-up.

* Persons in this business generation position will aim to achieve the goals of the Company relative to segment, product mix and shipments.

Attributes of Candidates for this Position:

Positive personality, Healthy Vitality, Clear Voice, Reliable, Prompt, Courteous to Others, Must be Coachable, Computer Literate, possess and exude a Can-do attitude, willing to do what it takes to exceed customer expectations; and is willing to be held accountable. Security knowledge of products and proper installation is a plus!

Process Responsibility may include:
        Execute Marketing Tasks
        Phone
        E-mail
        Lead Qualification
        Proposals
        Presentations
        Quotes
        New Customer Training on how to do business with the company
        Customer Technical Training
        Co-selling with Distributors or Manufacturers vendors
        Customer Care in the Field

Measures: Will include but are not limited to: Numbers of targets, number of qualified leads, number of proposals, number of presentations, number of quotes, number of orders entered x dollars, GPM Profit Margin %, returns, territory growth, and personal development via educational classes or courses completed.

GOALS will be established and issued and reviewed quarterly.

Persons in this position support by their actions the Company's proactive success foundation triangle comprised of Vision, Company Culture, Marketing & Sales, Operations, Training & Documentation.

Among the many considerations related to creating a sales and marketing position is to determine if the existing organization has the time and expertise necessary to support the position. Selection training and supervision takes a huge amount of time and commitment. If you think that you are too busy now to handle all of the business, wait until a dedicated sales pro starts pulling in new customers!

You will need to develop a fundamental shift in your business plan prioritization in order to be able to jump outside the box of your existing paradigm! Low profit activities that may have been previously eating up big chunks of your time and resources need to be reallocated to the back burner in order to accommodate the high profit priorities being created by the sales driven marketing plan.

Do you have the right environment that will support and develop the sales and marketing function in your organization?

What we mean by "environment" is whether or not you or someone on your staff will have the management skills necessary to lead and train a new team member into a new position and be successful. The following management leadership model while somewhat dated, still lends itself to the creation of the training and position management methodology that you need to develop to lead a successful sales and marketing function. We think it is very applicable to small business with it's typically "hands on" management style.

Situational Leadership

This is a term that can be applied generically to a style of leadership, but that also refers to a recognized, and useful, leadership model. In simple terms, a situational leader is one who can adopt different leadership styles depending on the situation. Most of us do this anyway in our dealings with other people: we try not to get angry with a nervous colleague on their first day, we chase up tasks with some people more than others because we know they'll forget otherwise.

But Ken Blanchard, the management guru best known for the "One Minute Manager" series, and Paul Hersey created a model for Situational Leadership in the late 1960's that allows you to analyze the needs of the situation you're dealing with, and then adopt the most appropriate leadership style. It's proved popular with managers over the years because it passes the two basic tests of such models: it's simple to understand, and it works in most environments for most people. The model doesn't just apply to people in leadership or management positions: we all lead others at work and at home.

LEADERSHIP BEHAVIOR

Blanchard and Hersey characterized leadership style in terms of the amount of direction and of support that the leader gives to his or her followers, and so created a simple grid:

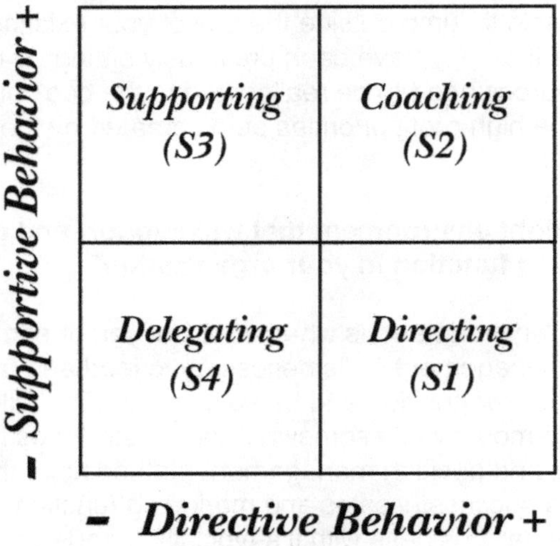

	Supporting *(S3)*	**Coaching** *(S2)*
	Delegating *(S4)*	**Directing** *(S1)*

Supportive Behavior + / − (vertical axis)

− Directive Behavior +

S1 Directing Leaders define the roles and tasks of the 'follower', and supervise them closely. Decisions are made by the leader and announced, so communication is largely one-way.

S2 Coaching Leaders still define roles and tasks, but seeks ideas and suggestions from the follower. Decisions remain the leader's prerogative, but communication is much more two-way.

S3 Supporting Leaders pass day-to-day decisions, such as task allocation and processes, to the follower. The leader facilitates and takes part in decisions, but control is with the follower.

S4 Delegating Leaders are still involved in decisions and problem solving, but control is with the follower. The follower decides when and how the leader will be involved.

Effective leaders are versatile in being able to move around the grid according to the situation, so there is no one right style. However, we tend to have a preferred style, and in applying Situational Leadership you need to know which one that is for you.

DEVELOPMENT LEVEL

Clearly the right leadership style will depend very much on the person being led - the follower - and Blanchard and Hersey extended their model to include the Development Level of the follower. They said that the leader's style should be driven by the Competence and Commitment of the follower, and came up with four levels:

D4   High Competence - High Commitment
Experienced at the job, and comfortable with their own ability to do it well. May even be more skilled than the leader.

D3   High Competence - Variable Commitment
Experienced and capable, but may lack the confidence to go it alone, or the motivation to do it well / quickly

D2   Some Competence - Low Commitment
May have some relevant skills, but won't be able to do the job without help. The task or the situation may be new to them.

D1   Low Competence - Low Commitment
Generally lacking the specific skills required for the job in hand, and lacks any confidence and / or motivation to tackle it.

Development Levels are also situational. I might be generally skilled, confident and motivated in my job, but would still drop into Level D1 when faced, say, with a task requiring skills I don't possess. For example, lots of managers are D4 when dealing with the day-to-day running of their department, but move to D1 or D2 when dealing with a sensitive employee issue.

SITUATIONAL LEADERSHIP

You can see where this is going. Blanchard and Hersey said that the Leadership Style (S1 - S4) of the leader must correspond to the Development level (D1 - D4) of the follower - and it's the leader who adapts.

For example, a new person joins your team and you're asked to help them through the first few days. You sit them in front of a PC, show them a pile of invoices that need to be processed today, and push off to a meeting. They're at level D1, and you've adopted S4. Everyone loses because the new person feels helpless and demotivated, and you don't get the invoices processed.

On the other hand, you're handing over to an experienced colleague before you leave for a holiday. You've listed all the tasks that need to be done, and a set of instructions on how to carry out each one. They're at level D4, and you've adopted S1. The work will probably get done, but not the way you expected, and your colleague despises you for treating him like an idiot. But swap the situations and things get better. Leave detailed instructions and a checklist for the new person, and they'll thank you for it. Give your colleague a quick chat and a few notes before you go on holiday, and everything will be fine.

By adopting the right style to suit the follower's development level, work gets done, relationships are built up, and most importantly, the follower's development level will rise to D4, to everyone's benefit.

We have been through a number of management training programs where the situational management model was taught and have found it to be useful for program development.   To make Situational Leadership work, you need to go through a training program, where you'll learn about how to operate effectively in all the Leadership Styles, and how to determine the Development Level of others. You can find these guys online and they will be happy to tell you all about their training programs.

You can also get the basics from Ken Blanchard's "Leadership and the One Minute Manager."

* You must have a written marketing plan for the creation and management of the new position!
* Employee recruiting, screening and selection should be on top of your action plans list.
* You have identified the perfect candidate to man your sales department – or have you?

EMPLOYEE SCREENING

When the hiring process, includes interviewing and a suitable screening of all applicants, it enables employers to create an efficient and more diverse workforce. The more thorough the planning process a company puts into these pre-hire initial employment steps, the greater the likelihood of finding good employees and the lower the possibility of future employment litigation.

All companies should provide applicants with standard employment applications, review resumes and conduct interviews. If you do not have your own human resource professionals and employment recruiters on staff, you really should look into outsourcing these valuable services and use personnel trained in conducting pre-employment interviews. It is their core competency and probably not yours!

Background investigations must not rely on only local checks, as many court jurisdictions may not be tied into state record systems automatically. While it may have changed, as of the year 2000, criminal records in New York City must be conducted separately for all 5 boroughs to obtain a city-wide record check on an applicant.

Employment records with gaps of time that cannot be verified should result in a huge red flag for hiring managers and must be resolved before you invest your time and money with a new employee. Unfortunately, many businesses rely on inadequate practices for background screening of potential employees. Employers without a plan who choose to "wing" their way through, end up all too often making quick hasty hiring decisions to fill a position and end up repenting at leisure when all sorts of personality and productivity problems surface. A false sense of security causes them to make common mistakes that can leave them exposed to even some costly litigation exposure.

You definitely should not rely merely on the applicant's statements in the application, resume and during the face-to-face interview process. Because, while your applicant may not outright tell you fabrications, important information about his or her background may get left out. If you fail to ask specific direct questions about the information on the application and in interviews, some may feel vague answers or omissions are acceptable.

If you just asked a question that requires a "yes or no" answer and the applicant rambles off in another direction, there is a red flag on the play!

Some unethical individuals will have few misgivings about misrepresenting the truth if they are desperate enough to get hired. Relying on the applicant to provide comprehensive, accurate information may leave you without the information that you need to make an intelligent decision.

If you use an employment service you should rely on what the recruiters tell you. Up to a point!

Because independent or even in-house recruiters perform a number of valuable services, it may be easy for the boss to step away from responsibilities in the hiring process and let the recruiter do the work and make the hard decisions. But remember recruiters; especially independent service companies are in the business of placement, not research.

While they may perform some background activities such as confirming academic degrees or past employment, recruiters don't offer the comprehensive background checks that can insulate your business from potential liability. In fact, standard language in the agreement that you signed with them will likely absolve them of any future liability.

Some companies have adopted the practice of making hiring decisions by committee or if your company is a Partnership, often all of the partners are involved in important hiring decisions. If a candidate looks good on paper, interviews well, and is viewed positively by the interviewing team, a vote settles the matter. While personality and interview presentation skills matter, you should remember that every person that you hire could eventually impact your entire operation.

Your team of interviewers can confirm that the applicant has the appropriate skills and traits for the position and a professionally conducted background check offers a critical verification that the judgment to select the candidate is the right one.

We don't want to be fear mongers here but making poor hiring decisions can put you at risk for all kinds of bad things that can happen. If you are a business that sends service technicians into other peoples businesses and homes, you absolutely must trust your employees 100% that they will not do anything illegal or immoral in the course of their employment that might result in you getting sued or at a minimum end up with a damaged reputation.

Did you know that statistics overwhelmingly demonstrate that any company could be at risk for making bad hiring decisions, and case law combined with jury awards support the argument that you simply cannot afford to ignore the risk?

According to some recent studies we found:

"Research conducted by the Society for Human Resource Management shows that 50 percent of all resumes and applications contain fabrications."

"The U.S. Department of Commerce estimates that employee theft causes 33 percent of all business failures."

"According to Bureau of Justice statistics, workplace violence accounts for 18 percent of all violent crimes."

"Under the legal doctrine of negligent hiring or retention, an employer has the duty to protect Its employees, clients and the public from injuries caused by employees whom the employer knows or "should have known" pose a risk of harm to others. Likewise, an employer may "be held liable for failing to investigate," discharge or reassign an employee."

"Overall, 66 percent of negligent hiring trial cases result in jury awards averaging $600,000 in damages. And, the Workplace Violence Research Institute reports that the average jury award for civil suits on behalf of the injured is $3 million."

Beyond the many good reasons to screen out potentially bad employees, employers with comprehensive background screening programs also enjoy many other benefits. We think that you will find the following list to be very compelling reasons to do it right!

1. Do you need to comply with federal regulations?

For instance for those engaged in transportation and interstate commerce, the Department of Transportation (DOT) oversees drug and alcohol testing programs on mandated employees.

The DOT requires employers to conduct a pre-employment drug test and obtain a two-year drug/alcohol test history. Additional regulations set forth by the DOT require employers to monitor their employees on an ongoing basis. DOT employers who fail to conduct this screening are subject to penalty fines. Fines if assessed, record-keeping fines can begin at $500 per day, and the fine for knowingly falsifying records can be $5,000.

Even though you are not under the auspices of federal control due to government contracts, you are under the requirement to make sure that your employees who operate your motor vehicles do so in a sober and conservative manner. You really need to know if an employee has a history of DWI or excessive motor vehicle offences that will likely drive up your insurance costs through the roof! Furthermore, you should have a program in place for annual DMV checks and counsel those that are putting you in peril.

2. Better attendance and lower turnover

A number of studies have been published that conclude that employers who conduct thorough background screening, including reference checking, experience better employee attendance rates and lower turnover. In addition, employers may see reduced healthcare and workers' compensation costs.

Costs associated with healthcare benefits, job-related accident frequency and resulting workers' compensation claims, have been shown to be directly related to background screening. There is a correlation between your claim frequency and hiring the best overall employees because it makes a difference in terms of attitude, safety and performance. When a drug free workplace program is also in place, you may be able to experience even greater cost savings.

Some safety experts recommend that employers should conduct a postconditional job offer workers' compensation search on applicants for jobs that require manual labor, standing for long periods of time or performing other duties that can lead to stress injuries such as chronic back pain. Your workers compensation insurer can also index the employees name and view prior claims in the event any new injury claim is filed while in your employ.

Fraud associated with workers' compensation claims, especially in regards to back, repetitive motion and other chronic pain complaints that are difficult to measure, is well documented.

3. Less theft

Overall, employers who conduct background screening experience fewer incidents of employee theft, fraud, embezzlement and shrinkage. London House, a company specializing in conducting psychological testing for employee honesty, determined a number of years ago that screening may reveal past theft or other criminal behavior, possibly preventing a bad hire. But also, having a solid background-screening program sends a message to potential employees. It demonstrates that an employer is concerned about who has access to financial or material assets and that the company will take appropriate action if necessary.

Honest people want to work with other honest people!

4. Less litigation

Background screening enables an employer not to hire a potentially bad employee, reducing the risk of accidents, criminal activity and violence—all of which may result in litigation. This is important if you ever have to defend yourself from a negligent hiring litigation. This can occur when someone claims that one of your employees through either direct action or negligence was the proximate cause of some injury to them. Have you ever said; "Boy if I just knew then what I know now, I wouldn't have ever hired him"!

Your screening program can help to demonstrate that you took reasonable measures to investigate the employee's background pre-hire. Consequently, exposure to a courtroom trial, bad publicity and hefty penalties is greatly reduced. It is called reasonable care.

5. Confirm an applicant is whom he or she claims to be

Now as never before, identity theft is a common problem. Employers must ensure that a potential employee is who they claim to be. Confirm an applicant's social security number by running a check on whether or not the number is valid by the screening company. In addition, a critical post-hire check is the I-9 verification, which must be conducted within three days of an employee starting his or her job. This search allows an employer to know whether or not a person can legitimately work in the United States.

A number of new programs have surfaced allowing employers to verify identity by calling INS and providing the persons name and social security number. A number of private companies can also allow you to conduct an outsourced check on all of your current employees for eligibility. We don't want to scare you, but there are a lot of people out there running around with false or "borrowed" identification.

6. More productive and better-qualified employees

The more you do to evaluate and qualify your job applicants through inter-views, reference checking or back-ground screening, the better its overall workforce will be. And, the greater the depth and "bench strength" you have, the better your overall productivity and performance can be.

When you screen your applicants, you're more likely to find qualified em-ployees for your open positions. Previous employment, education and professional verifications are just the beginning when determining whether an applicant will appropriately fit your needs.

You must protect everyone you employ by checking the criminal histories of applicants. If you knowingly hire ex-offenders with violent backgrounds or participate in work release programs to fill positions, don't be surprised when a lot of other good employees leave. Think about it, would you want to work at a company who hires felons? Would you want your kids to work there?

Employers who fail to exercise due diligence in their hiring practices risk hiring criminals at the very worst and unqualified workers at the least. They also risk workplace violence, theft and litigation.

Companies that experience an incident of workplace violence are exposed to several potential legal issues, including inadequate security, negligent hiring, negligent retention, and negligent supervision. Companies can take two basic steps to mitigate these risks: implementing an applicant screening process and a prevention program. The applicant screening process should aim to identify and weed out potential problems.

All job applicants should be required to take a drug test, and they should also be subjected to criminal background checks, credit checks, public-filing checks, driver's license checks, educational background checks, verification of previous employment, and reference checks. Any applicant who misrepresents or lies about his qualifications should raise a red flag. Did you know that only 35% of employers do a background check? You do, right?

Your company should consult with an attorney to make sure they have covered all the bases during this process. The prevention program should emphasize periodic employee training about the company's workplace violence policies and rules. A zero-tolerance policy for threats and intimidation and a clear and unambiguous definition of unacceptable behavior especially involving sexual harassment are essential.

Ensure all applicants complete the prior criminal conviction section on the employment application. If the applicant checks "yes" to the question of prior criminal conviction on their application, instruct your managers to contact a superior or the owner for direction on whether to hire or not hire this applicant. Do not hire applicants that are participating in a criminal work release program, drug halfway house or any similar program.

The background investigation should include criminal history and prior employment verification. Background investigations should be conducted by a reputable outside agency. Get their references and check them out before you hire the service.

Joey D's Lesson Learned – Background Checks

Hiring the right Sales Person for the first time can be perilous, a total guess, and a hope or just plain luck! The first time I hired a sales person my gut lied to me! This fellow was a neat dress-for-success disciple, clean-shaven, with meticulous personal habits, polite, and spoke well. He showed up five minutes before the interview, had notes and questions written in a daily planner and a fresh copy of an impressive resume.

The energy he flashed at the interview was appropriate and his basic range of conversation about security products revealed a working knowledge of electronic security and a novice level at mechanical hardware but he asked good questions and seemed willing to learn. More importantly because he was in a related business albeit as a manufacturer direct sales person whose company was purchased by one of the conglomerates and his division dissolved. He talked the talk about area accounts and claimed relationships and contacts. BONUS the guy had contacts!

When he asked for a salary less than I was planning on offering, this seemed to good to be true! We were even in violent agreement on benefits, expenses and vacation. It was a can't miss deal, so he was hired on the spot! Remember the too good to be true? I should have respected the old adage!

Was I ever wrong! Upon the news of being offered the position he said he was taking a two-week vacation to clear his head and would be available immediately after that for training. No problem, let's have the guy start with a clean slate, plus that would give me time to line up what we needed him to learn. "We'll work with it", I said.

This guy was the best actor of all time! Much to my chagrin he saved his best for the interview! This enthusiastic interviewee with the air of confidence and independence became an overnight high maintenance vehicle!

But still I decided to wade through the transition for if he produced, putting up with personal peccadilloes would be an okay price to pay. Wrong again!

This guy had an "old book" of contacts, and most of his business friends moved on! He was unable to make new contacts and was too aggressive with prospects, to the point he was unable to get past the gatekeeper on many occasions! What a nightmare...a great looking, sweet talking guy that can't get an appointment let alone make a sale!

Then he complained about having no real leads. Then he complained the leads we gave him (existing clients) never needed anything. Since he was not selling and making a minimum base plus expenses, he was getting edgy after just a few weeks.

My belief in his persona and my trust in his ability were fading fast. It was time to make a field trip with this fellow. Digging deeper, it was learned he was sarcastic when someone said "no". This is bad. "No" usually means the timing is not right or you have not given me enough information. He took no as a personal affront and got nasty in front of me with the prospect. I'm not a fan of cold calls and here is a good demonstration why! Nevertheless the only good news was we were visiting prospects he lined up.

It was quickly realized this guy had personal problems and issues preventing him from doing the job. His divorce, which had come up in the interview, and perceived to be a renewed motivator to kick his income to a higher level, was incorrect. He was not adjusting to his new life alone. According to him, the divorce was not his idea. To add insult to injury, his ex-spouse was the real breadwinner and he was actually dependent on her to maintain the lifestyle that provided him the comfort that breeds that air of confidence. After riding with him in casual conversation it was obvious he was a bitter man negative towards woman and just awful for my business.

After the ride, my query to him was, "Do you think this position with my company will help you get to where you want to go? He looked down at the ground and said, "No, not really. It is harder than expected, and my hearts not in it." Accepting his resignation was more humane than firing him. But this proved a point, it is easy to get fooled, there has to be more than a "gut" check to hiring sales people.

There are many Human resource tools to help you "scientifically" evaluate potential sales people. One effective tool is the Predictive Index survey, a managerial assessment tool that provides insight into the natural workplace behaviors of prospective and existing employees – resulting in improved hiring decisions, team performance, overall communication, and workforce productivity. You can evaluate strengths, weaknesses and tendencies of people by type. It has proven to be accurate and helped me avoid some bad hires!

The other key missing part of the puzzle leading to the failure of this sales candidate was the fact that a thorough background check might have revealed problems in previous employment!

Hire in haste and repent at leisure! We have included some tools that can help you to formalize your hiring procedures, become consistent with your questions and get the expected answers from an applicant.

But back to the current issue! Gaetano was ready to hire! Where will the right person be found? Should an ad be placed in the local newspaper? Should it be posted on the Internet at a pay site or unpaid listing? Should the general message be filtered through the local trade that we are looking? All good questions! So after writing each question down, and careful consideration, he decided each and everyone can be effective, but the local newspaper was the first choice.

Without giving away too much information, Gaetano began to write, remembering this is an advertisement, something to catch attention and offer some differentiation, not just another "Salesperson Wanted" generic ad.

NEW Business Generation Manager Position in Anywhere City, USA

Looking for a Great Opportunity in a HOT Industry? Join a company with a proven track record that is on-the-grow and looking for YOU! We have more prospects than we can develop! If you are coachable, personable, energetic, and outgoing with a vivacious appetite for succe$$ with presentation skills, captivating persona and looking for an opportunity to earn and learn and make money you deserve. Send your resume to: me@myemail.com The Ad was placed for the weekend editions, usually the most effective due to the larger readership. He figured if someone saw the ad, knew him and had someone in mind, he'd get referrals too.

What else is important for this project? How do you go about developing a consistent approach needed for the process of interviewing and hiring the perfect candidate? To start with, you need to identify the list of attributes needed for success in this job and create the ideal profile.

Next, you need a tool to grade the applicants against the profile. That is the purpose of developing the interview guide. You have to be systematic and ask everyone the same questions in order to gauge the replies.

INTERVIEW GUIDE

This candidate has completed the Employment Application. You have reviewed the information and invited this individual for a live interview

The Position: Inside & Telephone Sales Representative

Description: The Inside & Telephone SALES REPRESENTATIVE POSITION at THIS COMPANY is a proactive business generation position

Attributes of Candidates for this Position include but are not limited to: Healthy Vitality, Positive Personality, Clear Voice, Reliable, Prompt, Courteous to Others, Must be Coachable, Computer Literate, possess and exude a Can-do attitude, willing to do what it takes to exceed customer expectations, security products knowledge

Do you feel this list of attributes accurately reflects you?

What interview questions would you ask?

*   Persons in this position are responsible for consistent, accurate and timely execution of all sales processes. Tell us your experience.
*   Give examples of a process or you have executed successfully.
*   Persons in this position are accountable for results by the Owner of the Business. Are you results oriented? Give examples!
*   Give example of the best person you ever reported to and tell why.
*   Persons in this position are expected to work within the paper and electronic operating systems of the Company. Can you...?
*   Are you computer literate? Do you own a PC, Laptop or MAC?

Attributes of Candidates for this Position:

Healthy Vitality, Positive Personality, Clear Voice, Reliable, Prompt, Courteous to Others, Must be Coach-able, Computer Literate, possess and exude a Can-do attitude, willing to do what it takes to exceed customer expectations.

Process Responsibility for this Position includes:
>   Floor/Showroom/Counter Sales
>   All Related Paperwork
>> Quotes
>> Work Orders
>> Special Non-Stock Product Orders
>> Invoices
>   New Customer Set-up
>   Phone Management for Prospecting & Closing
>   Update Product Catalogs
>   Written Proposals
>   Develop Sales Presentations
>   Execute Sales Presentation
>   Floor/Showroom/Counter Sales Display Maintenance

Personal Development and Business Performance GOALS will be established, distributed and reviewed quarterly.

Business Measures are typically reviewed weekly, monthly and quarterly. Measures may include: Numbers of phone calls initiated, number of floor demonstrations, number of proposals, quotes, and orders. Total gross sales, GPM (Gross Profit Margin), Training Classes attended.

Make your standardized list and ask a number of "open" key questions to draw out details of your candidates reasoning and thought process: Along with the previous examples, ask some of these.

"Give examples of detail oriented tasks you have routinely executed".

"Give an example of a negative situation where your intervention and attributes resulted in a satisfactory result for your employer, the customer and you".

Or these

- Why do you consider yourself a person driven to achieve or exceed goals?
- Have you ever participated on a Sports Team?

- What hobbies interest you?
- What are your long-term life goals?
- If you had $500,000,000 what would you do with it?
- How do you view employment in terms of time. Do you look to be at this Company as a one year, three years, or career position?
- If you had your chance to do everything all over again, what one thing would you do first?
- Why are you the best candidate to fill this position?

Make a list of winning answers and you now have a profile for the successful candidate!

Always thank them for taking the time to participate in the interview. Inform them you will get back to you with an answer within 24 Hours (or a specific time frame). Now comes the really hard part of making the perfect selection!

Date	None Better Hire NOW	Better than Average	Just ENOUGH	Below Average	NO WAY
Positive Can-Do Person					
Organized					
Self-Starter					
Team Player					
Computer Literate					
Internet Savvy					
Listens Well					
Aura of Confidence					
Accountable					
Candidate NAME:			Position:	Inside Sales	
Notes:					

Keep track of everyone you interview by completing an evaluation form. This is really helpful if you interview many applicants.

Amanda checks off the Bread Aisle as now
secure and scores Mr. B's camera install
style and technique a 10!

Chapter 14   The training program you need to insure success!

Documentation & Training

Joey D's Lessons From Successes- Training Issues

Have you ever wondered why your employees are not consistent? Do you wonder how they can come to work and just go through the motions? Do you wonder if they will ever get it? What has this got to do with transitioning from a reactive to a proactive marketing and sales plan?

The answer is without proper documentation and training your people will not know exactly what to do! Never assume people you hire will learn the details by mimicking the actions of the owner or other employees. Acting the part in a business is not the same as being a living part of the business!

How well you document the processes and procedures in your business, in all aspects, will determine the potential speed trainees can learn. Your goal in training is to get people productive as fast as possible! The faster they learn the less likely you are to lose money.

Documentation ought not be boring!

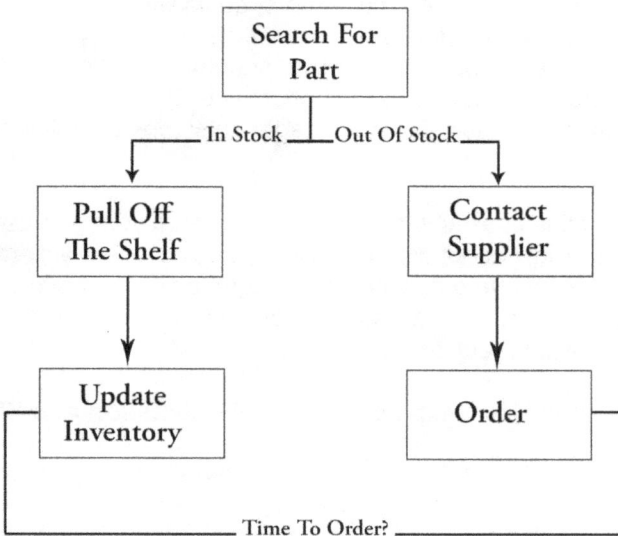

```
                        ┌──────────────┐
                        │  Search For  │
                        │    Part      │
                        └──────────────┘
              ___ In Stock ___│___ Out Of Stock ___
             │                                      │
             ▼                                      ▼
     ┌──────────────┐                      ┌──────────────┐
     │   Pull Off   │                      │   Contact    │
     │  The Shelf   │                      │   Supplier   │
     └──────────────┘                      └──────────────┘
             │                                      │
             ▼                                      ▼
     ┌──────────────┐                      ┌──────────────┐
     │   Update     │                      │    Order     │
     │  Inventory   │                      │              │
     └──────────────┘                      └──────────────┘
        │                                          │
        └────────────── Time To Order? ───────────┘
```

Depicting the processes in a step-by-step pictorial manner rather than just word descriptions is great way to communicate your message.

You should write ordinary processes and procedures for ordinary people. When they execute as planned, you can attain extraordinary results. If you write extraordinary processes and procedures for ordinary people, your result will likely not be what you want.

Documentation is critical, training important to your success in minimizing risk and preventing loss.

The Sales and Marketing Training Program

What every security hardware-marketing sales manager needs to know.

Study Tools:

1.   Competitive Advantage-Fixing Small Business Security And Safety Problems (textbook)

Competitive Advantage - Where you can learn how the loss prevention policies, procedures and programs used by large international corporations can be adapted to fit any sized organization…even yours! Can your business gain a Competitive Advantage through a Loss Prevention Program? Every business with employees, retail customers, deals with cash and inventory; factors in "shrink" as an ordinary business write-off. This "planned loss" can be greatly minimized through proper loss prevention tactics and tools. The result is an increase in dollars to the bottom line. Businesses that generate more profits gain a Competitive Advantage! This book will tell you how to do it.

The purpose of this book is to teach you about what your end user customer needs to know about controlling losses due to theft, violent crime and claims. Your knowledge puts you in the unique position above your peers at competitor companies, to advise your customers about the best and most cost effective ways to reduce their losses.

2.   Marketing Roadmap PowerPoint Presentation And Workbook

The material consists of a Power Point presentation and workbook that shows the sales pro some basic tools to use that are commonly used to gather customer information. The presentation emphasizes what you need to know about the equipment and systems that you will be selling.

3.   Company Employee Handbook

Every company needs to have an employee handbook to identify rules and policies that must be followed as a condition of employment. You will learn by reviewing your own company programs and policies how similar information should be available to assist you in the process of showing our customer's methods and products for reducing risk exposure.

Overview of Presentation:

Knowledge Base Modules

- Business exposure to loss
- Business losses by type
- Reasons that losses occur
- Impact of business losses
- Loss Exposure Quiz

You will gain knowledge about the types of losses that your customers are experiencing and be able to create a security hardware product solution that blocks your customers loss exposure and works to prevent future losses from occurring. Crime losses are discussed by type and include the reasons that are commonly attributed to why the loss occurred and what can be done to reduce the risk of re-occurrence.

This segment details the impact of losses on business profits and the reason that an action plan must be developed by the business. You will learn that the costs associated with the purchase of security hardware and systems are often available by using the systems that you sell to recover lost profits that the business owner has been walking away from and writing off as a cost of doing business.

- Concept of "shrinkage" and inventory loss
- Employee theft
- Customer/shoplifting losses
- Fraud
- Delivery theft
- Cost Variance
- Shrinkage Quiz

This module will provide you with in depth knowledge of common business crime losses, how they occur and what the common hardware, procedures and policies do to impact the loss.

- Post incident security response
- Business response to loss incidents

- Immediate Concerns
- Post incident planning
- Resources to use
- Loss Response Quiz

Security products companies such as yours are often the next to be called after a crime is reported to the police and the role that you have is being the key responder to securing the property after a burglary, robbery, property damage or other crime incident. This module will teach you about the resources and tools needed to quickly button down your customer's property after an incident and provide the time needed to survey and analyze what happened in order to create your proposal to upgrade customer security.

Security circles and basic defensive practices

- Overview of "Holistic" loss prevention theory
- Interaction of systems, hardware, procedures and policies
- Prevention hardware barriers and what they do and don't do.
- Identifying "Best, Better or Good" levels of response to an existing exposure.
- Quiz

This section provides more advanced skills to learn that addresses how systems, policies and procedures work together as a whole entity. The process will teach the new sales pro to help your customers identify the level of hardware resources to apply against a loss exposure depending on the value of assets to be protected.

Rules Policies and Procedure

- Key elements of a written policy
- Banking and Cash Controls
- Security Policies
- Safety Program Interaction with business losses
- Resources
- Policies and Procedures Quiz

This segment will explain the purpose of policies and procedures in business establishments and what the results are when losses occur in their absence. The sales pro will learn to use the absence of policies as a predictor of future losses due to increased opportunity.

Conducting Surveys

- Using surveys to identify loss exposure

- Approved formats
- Interpreting Survey results
- Linking exposures to the barriers and programs you have to offer.
- Resources to use
- Survey Quiz

The key to every sales proposal is to discover not only what the customer thinks that they want in a given loss exposure scenario but also what is actually going to work based on the site survey and examination of existing barriers and hardware. You will learn to ask the right questions that extract the important information you need to assemble your proposal and make the presentation.

Marketing the Holistic approach to end-users.

- Creating proposals
- Linking proposal elements to customer end-user ROI
- Creating urgency
- Prioritizing recommendations
- Quiz

The final segment ties all of your knowledge base together along with workable time line approaches to cre-ate proposals that sell.

Practical Knowledge Exercise

The practical exercise will involve a run through of a scenario that will determine if you are ready for the new challenges of the job. Ready, set, go!

Creating and monitoring your training program can be the most daunting and rewarding part of your leap from reactive to proactive marketing. Really, your success is mainly due to the quality and training of your employees at all levels of your business.

We want to again emphasize that many of the tasks of creating a marketing and sales program can be out-sourced with a measurable return on your investment! See more about this in Chapter 16.

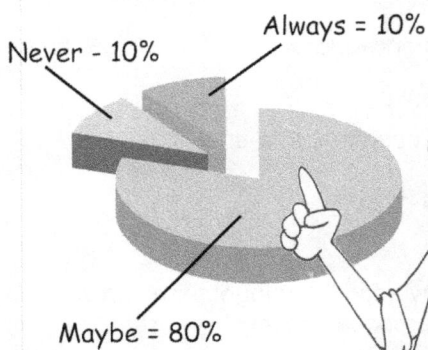

Ladder pro Mr. B hangs a high one!

Chapter 15   Measuring Your Success – Was It All Worth It?

The best way that we can express and measure success in our industry is to look at those who have taken a deep breath and through talent and tenacity changed the direction of their business to maximize their odds of success. They may be the exception that proves the rule that you can make organizational changes with careful thought and planning.

Transitioning from the "Locksmith" to "Security Director"

Steve Ehrlich started Reliable Lock & Key in Taunton, MA in the seventies. In the beginning products and services were mechanically based lock, key and safe related. While the market trend was a few years off, Steve viewed the advent of electric and electronic hardware as a key to the future growth of the company and began acquiring the knowledge and expertise to add these products and services to clients and prospects.

Steve's son Michael grew up in the business and was one of the youngest technicians to achieve the CML (certified master locksmith) credential. Mike also had a vision of acquiring a total channel knowledge and joined the ranks of the nation's leading wholesaler of security products as Regional Manager. Mike was an astute observer and quickly understood the fulfillment functions and operations required to produce on time delivery as well as remaining profitable. Recruiting, hiring and training was also part of the responsibility and invaluable experience was also gained. Next Mike went to work for Medeco High Security Locks, acquiring understanding of strategic alliance partners and relationships between the Manufacturers, Wholesale Distributors and Dealers.

Mike returned to Reliable and it was time for re-tooling to prepare a much broader scope of business, providing an integrated security product for existing clients and new customers.

The business had a strong customer base but clients viewed the business as a locksmith service company, not a security sales and service company. Changes to the company was driven in part by vision and on part because customers were using competitors to install access control or CCTV equipment, customers originally calling Reliable for locks were locked on to a perception and thought if the company for that type of business only.

Time for some marketing! Mike decided to implement a marketing plan where promoting the image of their security business by positioning their role as "Security Directors" for their client would enable the introduction of related products and services.

The advantage to the client is cost reduction by using a "single source." Leveraging the trust already earned plus doing business with a reliable company that understood the physical security needs of the business as it relates to doors, hardware and key holders makes integrating security equipment such as Alarms, Closed Circuit Television, Electronic Access Control to increase the safety and security of the people and property as an addition to the mechanical hardware make sense.

The transition from locksmith to Security Director is not simply a name change to the business and a new title for the cardholder. The real value of the role of the Security Director is involvement in the planning stages, not in the reactive procedures of handling security issues after the fact. Earning the invitation to be involved in the early planning stages of customers' building renovation or new construction projects is the target scenario. Combining knowledge with needs, the role of the Security Director is then to identify solutions that will match the flow of traffic as it relates to security and safety.

The selection of products that will meet the budget, style and operational needs of the client are better decided in the new construction phases. Savings in labor and maintenance as well as planning the preservation of the equipment to perform as intended is well worth it for the client

There is some marketing and selling savvy required to be considered in this vital role, but often it is provided by educating the customer about solutions, whether policy, procedure or products. In addition it is also a terrific opportunity to introduce ongoing service programs for additional revenues.

The decision to take this track was soul searching. The "tech" in most lock based business owners actually prevents them from making the decision to put down the tool box, take off the "uniform" step out of the van and put on a suit and tie and mix it up with the people invariably making the decisions on building security. The transition is painful but exhilarating!

Mike & Steve decided to leverage the business relationships with the client base and planned to contact key accounts with personal involvement. They understand while the nature of the security business is hands-on, the high-tech of the business requires instruction and training and in essence communicating with the customer directly is high touch, satisfying that innate need to be involved and that is what can make the difference.

Customers trusted the Ehrlich's, so taking the role of Sales/Security Director made the most sense. In order to assume these positions, another dramatic move was required. For many lock based business owners hiring someone to take over the daily operations of the business would be unlikely but to free up the resources best equipped to contact customers and tell the security solutions story, it had to be done. Other key positions were identified, defined and filled. A full time estimator turned out to be a key hire and further increased the productivity of the business.

More on Marketing the Business....
Aside from increasing their contact with existing customers, both Ehrlich's developed relationships with security consultants too. Security Consultants are typically "up" on policy, procedure, laws and have product knowledge, however with the rapid introduction of new technology, new products and related integration challenges a lot can be learned from partnering with trusted security professionals to provide a better security overall product for clients.

Today ISI is a leading systems integrator in the Southeastern New England Region. In the beginning revenues were obviously derived from a lock and key service company, today electronic security dominates and the transition successful.

A professional Sales Team in addition to the technical expertise - Integrated Security Systems, Miami FL

Owner Jeff Nunberg transitioned one of the most successful safe and lock businesses in the Greater Miami Area into one of the nations leading regional providers of safety and security solutions. Jeff says advanced technology and exceptional customer service are the hallmarks of Integrated Security Systems, Miami FL – A nationally recognized security solutions provider with one of the finest reputations in the industry.

Jeff notes that in the early nineties it was obvious the future funding of security budgets were targeting investment in electronic security products and services to control access and increase security and not the traditional strict reliance on mechanical hardware and key systems. He decided to be part of the future and started the transition. First closing two locations, then purchasing an industrial building capable of housing a much larger operation, then finally closing his last lock store, forgoing the retail business. During the transition period, acquiring the skill sets, training, licensing, permits, certifications and personnel did not happen over night. Today while mechanical locks are still part of the solution, the company excels at mechanical and electronic integration for an improved add value for its clients. With over sixty employees it is a long way from its roots as a local safe and lock shop.

Jeff is a visionary, and back then saw the market trends early and developed a strategy to head into the next century as a leading firm and not just another player or business that simply rode the wave. Integrated Security

Systems serves Fortune 100, 500 companies as well as mid-size and smaller commercial, institutional clients that need to protect personnel, secure physical assets, control access, reduce potential liability and implement an effective risk management system. A professional Sales Team in addition to the technical expertise, product knowledge, strategic relationships with vendors and an open mind to continued change keep ISS at the top of their game.

Integrated Security Systems combines the latest in technology – including an advanced phone processing system, computerized dispatching and internet communications and ordering capabilities – with friendly, personal attention to clients' specific needs. Professional technicians are available 24-hours a day, seven days a week.

State-of-the-art security solutions including Access Control Systems, Closed Circuit Television Systems (CCTV), Intrusion Detection Systems, Fire Alarm and Life Safety Systems, UL Central Station Monitoring, Master Key Systems and Complete Commercial Locksmith Services are part of the integrated approach.

How does ISS market the business? In addition to a professional outside sales team, a terrific web site and a physical plant to impress, the business is active in various local and national trade and business associations, constantly networks with security professionals working for clients and target customers.

The transition over the years resulted in a dramatic reversal of good fortunes. The move from a successful lock and safe company to an integrated security company results in a business today doing under ten percent of its business in mechanical keys and locks and over ninety percent in electronic security a big change from fifteen years ago!

Captures the eye from the outside and blows you away on the inside!

Owners Mike Elsberry and Dee Kopczynski have led the transition from what began as a traditional local safe and lock business started by Mike's Father, is now a leading system integrator for security and safety to home automation. At **A&E Security and Electronic Solutions, McMinnville, Oregon**. The company provides Alarm monitoring, Alarms for intrusion and fire, home , business , Indoor wiring , Intercom systems , Lighting (exterior) Locks: home , business , Safes (combination and fire), Closed Circuit Television, Electronic access control, Speaker systems (in-wall, multi-room) and Vacuum systems!

The transition from a business located in two-bay former gas station, into one now in a modern design multi-story structure of 8,000 square feet, is a fair parallel of the business development too! The business is located in a small market and Mike's decision was to expand services and products to the existing market rather than try to string together multiple locations stretching into the bigger Portland market some sixty miles away.

From the time of the decision to expand the product and services offering to today, besides the physical plant, the most obvious change is in the business "mix". The dominance of electric and electronic products and related services are now in excess of eighty percent of the business, from a business that did ninety five percent mechanical just a dozen years ago!

Mike says in addition to deciding to change the mix and adding or developing related skill sets, acquiring licensing, certifications, and creating strategic alliances with vendors, the single most important aspect to the transition was a commitment to developing a sales organization. "Recruiting, hiring and training sales people to call on existing clients and to develop new customers took the business from a reactive reliable provider to a proactive customer focused company."

Dee says the internal commitment to excel at the dispatch and business fulfillment functions with documentation and ongoing training in the entire operations center is truly the enabler to growth. As partners, both have worked long hours, weekends and holidays, doing whatever it took to keep on the vision path, both say it was not easy and "We work hard at it every day, but we agree we have truly transitioned from a past with roots we are proud of to something our founders would also understand is the place the business had to go to be part of a terrific future".

So how did they market the business?

Location, location, location! Having a great location helps! Taking that location and building a New Structure that captures the eye from the outside and blows you away on the inside helps even more! Adding the afore-mentioned professional sales people to the location and building attributes makes the difference; and the recipe for success has a good base.

Communication is another important aspect to marketing your business. Joining local business association and community groups is a great networking tool and an opportunity to promote you and your business.

Choosing a strategic alliance with proactive key vendors helps build local co-identity with brand association. For instance people may recognize the

GE label and this adds credibility to A&E.

The name change from A&E Safe & Lock to A&E Security and Electronic Solutions is an example of marketing a message to potential clients in the business name itself. For people that know the business, A&E is still recognizable for those new prospects while they may not recognize the safe and lock aspects from the name itself, the appeal to consumers in search of electronic security is attempted and when prospects visit A&E or just call, they will either see or hear about the range of products and services.

Owner Mike Elsberry said with a Safe and Lock selling alarms to customers was an occasional thing, and even less so with people who did not know the business. The association of alarm and electronics was not an image within the mind of the customer when seeing Safe and Lock. Often safe and lock customers whether commercial, retail or residential sought those products and services elsewhere. In order to change the expectation of the customer who "knew" the business, sales people, local advertisement and direct mail helped communicate a broader security offering.

A name change isn't the only "magic" for A&E or anyone else, but the name change was a key ingredient in identifying and marketing the new brand.

Transition? How about continuous improvement!

Pinder's Security, St Catherine's Ontario is a fifth generation locksmith based company that truly defines transition and transformation from the hand crafted locks and keys of the 1800's when the business began, to a fully and totally integrated security company today.

Greg Pinder, President is an industrial engineer by degree and his skills in developing process, policies and procedures led to the "Pinder Approach" a comprehensive closed loop system that provides a great foundation for any customer to maximize their investment through correct application, development, installation and ongoing management of key and card access systems, hardware and electronic security as well as the ongoing maintenance to ensure lifetime expectancy performance of all components.

The Pinder locksmith business of old satisfied customers with outstanding service, and the fully integrated security package of today satisfies customers too. One major change today is the influence of the IT Manager in any security equipment or information management decision. Being able to comprehend then address the impact has meant an entire new dimension. Pinder's finds itself facilitating conversations between IT Departments and Manufacturers to develop software to meet the needs. That's a lot of work to secure the sale, but a necessary component of a totally integrated security provider.

It is the savvy to understand the customer needs and willingness to change the business to meet the needs that is a success ingredient at Pinder's. Constant education of employees and staff to training of key accounts is necessary to keep pace, and often driving the change. Greg Pinder says, "Providing a level of service that prevents your customer from ever wanting to look elsewhere is a basic tenet of our business." Pinder's superior documented program defines how-to steps every step of the way for the end user adds tremendous value and differentiation.

Another advantage is Pinder's Security capability of beginning a relationship with an end-user, literally from the ground up. A New Construction Contract Hardware Division begins many relationships, designing and developing the appropriate system application with a specialty staff of qualified professionals that understand the entire integration process. After acquiring appropriate projects, the Security Business personnel defines, designs, installs and begins implementing the ongoing service and operating programs, typically led off by a training program for the end-user.

Well known for decades as a mechanical locks and large master-key systems expert, Pinder's transition began as an early pioneer in electronic security, including electronic access controls, closed circuit television, lighting, and audio. In addition to a wonderful commercial, industrial, and institutional client list, Pinder's also does a terrific job in residential security, extending their Total Integrated approach. Greg said, "When commercial customers ask what we can do for security of their homes, we have an opportunity and really an obligation to serve them," A great web-site questionnaire can walk the homeowner through a series of instructions/questions and leads them to make security decisions beyond door knobs, deadbolts and keys. It is also very good for business according to Greg.

We believe that every business is capable of change. Managing your business outside of your self proscribed paradigm can be a scary consideration but one that has to be considered by any company owner who plans on staying in business for the foreseeable future.

The future will belong to the people who are able to perform an introspective analysis of their business assets and liabilities and turn their best positive attributes into a long-term business plan…AND execute the plan!

DARYL GOES TO CANADA TO SEE
HOW PINDER DOES IT & LEARNS
THAT THE MONEY LOOKS DIFFERENT!

Chapter 16

And Finally Famous Last Words

Chapter 16   And Finally Famous Last Words

The two central themes of this book are how to effectively transition from reactive to proactive marketing and sales, market your security hardware and services business and how to design your product offering to show a markedly different level of your services versus your competitors.

Differentiation is the key to breaking out of the clutter and having your target customers recognize the qualities that make you unique and make them want to do business with you.

Thoughts on Continuous change from JoeyD.

Thought one:

Can you see the day in your business when you will not have to purchase products for resale? If you are forced into an "installation and service only position" that is the reality, what steps are you taking in preparation? Installation, Repair and Preventative Maintenance Services can provide a handsome profit if you have lean management, the right business tools and the right technical staff and a fleet.

Thought Two:

Many of you are application experts, limited by growth due to a lack of capital to invest in people, buildings, logistics, etc. What if you leveraged your application expertise and transitioned your business into a Security Marketing & Sales Company and outsourced installation and service, perhaps by specific end-user type or size, and materials handling as well?

Would that add value to Suppliers and Manufacturers? You bet!

The economics change and just might be more favorable to your wallet.

Thought Three:

Should you consider "Application Selling" and become expert in an exclusive and particular area such as Truck Fleet Security, or Key Systems Management for Small Business, or Electronic Access Control for Jewelry Stores or Biometrics for Evidence Rooms, or Door Safety for Private Schools or Keyless Entry for the Home? All potentially lucrative areas with minimal if any competition?

DO YOU GET THE PICTURE?

If you do not continuously plan the change and implement proactively, your business must change to keep up the "status quo" and that might not serve your needs in a timely manner. Wouldn't you hate to be looking up to see down?

Consider the following.

Why would the words of Michael T. Dan be of interest to you? As Chairman, President & CEO of Brinks he is a powerful man in a terrific position with an impressive company and a whole lot of brand recognition. He recently said: "We will continue to grow our existing strong security businesses, focus on accelerating the growth of high-potential opportunities within those businesses, continue to exploit the cash flow, brand-building and other benefits of operating two premier businesses under the same flagship brand, and aggressively explore the expansion of the Brinks brand into suitable security-related businesses."

Is this why they are installing electronic access control systems of 3 to 5 doors test targeting commercial businesses in the Texas and Florida markets? Okay, so you say "not to worry, I don't do business there". What about after the "test"? Is your marketplace next?

While these jobs are not very large by any measure, typically nine to fifteen thousand dollars, they are very profitable and the "sweet spot" according to one of Brinks' technical EAC engineers. Is this your sweet spot too, the low hanging fruit? Maybe it is true, the big jobs are for prestige but the smaller ones are for cash flow.

Not too comforting is it? What are your options when confronted by intrusive competitive forces on what used to be your turf? You can do nothing and let the competition eat a part of your lunch or:

A.   Identify all of your "low hanging fruit" opportunities.
B.   Create a plan to identify potential customers who are the
        competitive target of opportunity.
C.   Beat out the Big Name boiler room sales competitor by
        preempting their game. Proactively grab the sales and profits that
        you are about to lose!

The Call to Action

Owning your own business is the American Dream. No one in America can guarantee you that you will succeed; in fact the statistics are overwhelmingly in favor of failure! To succeed in your security business today, even if you have been in business for a long time, you must have more than knowledge of your craft to survive. You must understand trends in security and the business of doing business. You must take the necessary actions to provide the products, services and solutions people want to buy.

If you are committed to a product offered strategy where you stand behind a sign and say this is what we do, this is what we've always done and that is all we are ever going to do, you have signed a business death certificate, it is just a question as to when the funeral will be. It is important to note, that this position may be okay for you. You may decide, "When I'm done doing it my way and I can no longer do it, I'm done. We'll just close the doors and that's it".

On the other hand if you are interested in maintaining your current life style, or if you are like most people and want to improve the quality of your life, whether that means more time or more money, or you just want to build a business someone else will buy, then you must take action to get to where you want to go.

Some business owners in our security hardware sector based businesses are proactively making moves to give their businesses a calculated opportunity for success and survival well into the future. You have read of a few in this book. It is your choice in what direction you take your business. The opinion of experts is if you do the same old things the same old way, you will not be as successful in a changing world. The steps you take are up to you. Strategy is doing the right things, Tactics are doing things right and Execution through operations will help you get there on time with the "right stuff".

Some will read this and say, "Hey My Business is doing just great. We just keep on "keeping on" and things seem all right, we're not making any changes." After all, this is a capitalist economic system and you can do what you want, but for those with even an inking of desire to change, we hope this book will inspire you to try.

The strictly mechanical locksmith based businesses and many alarm service providers as well, are challenged, there is no denying that. In this consumer driven world some people seek the security, quality, professionalism and attention to detail and the extremely important peace of mind they get dealing with a professional business that makes them feel safe. You have a head start because many of your customers already feel this way abut you. Reach out to them before they get in touch someone else!

You may have a solid base business and just need a new direction or you may have a business just looking for a plan. Either way if you just sit there and watch what happens or worse wonder "what just happened?", then you won't make anything happen….and that would be a tragedy.

Your call to action is really a personal check-up from the neck up. Do you like where you are today? Given your current course will you be happier in 5 years, in decline or out of business? Take action…Plan you work then work your plan!

To those that think change is simply too difficult given the resources you think are available, we need to make at least some effort at shameless promotion here. You and I know that many of you will not be capable of following the guidance in this book and actually make changes. You need to know that there are resources out there that can execute changes for you and are affordable because the return on investment planning pays for it in a measurable way.

Let's assume you have made a decision to take action….anything, something, everything! Where will you begin? Let's consider as follows:

After your neck up analysis you have decided that moving to a Proactive plan to grab the sales of your most profitable items is what you want to do. You have completed your SWOT organizational analysis and have determined that the technical expertise of your company is excellent but tuned in to doing a very good job at the tasks of what you are currently doing.

You have a good cash flow but spend too much money on labor and inventory maintenance to make a lot of your usual activities not very profitable. You are merely busy.

Consider how you are allocating your cash flow, what can you afford to do right now, next month, next quarter? You will need to develop a plan to gather the resources at hand and expand your expertise in the area of executing a sales and marketing driven expansion.

Your analysis has shown you that your existing people, as good as they are, will need NEW hands-on technical training to be able to productively handle the volume of sales that you expect from your new product initiatives. AND you do not have sales people ready to go to find new customers and drive the change in your paradigm! AND you have never hired or had to train a sales person and really do not know how you can learn to do all of that plus be concerned with the technical production side of the changes you want to make. DO not be discouraged, recognizing what you need to do is half the battle! Congratulations!

You need a place to start the process. You can either take it slow and focus on one product at a time or get Professional Help to make a quantum leap.

There are OUT SOURCE Pros that can help you plan then make the change by showing you how to or actually creating a marketing plan with a measurable return on investment to implement the retooling of your production activities toward the high profit products you want….a by product is identifying what low profit busy-work activities you should put on the back burner.

The Out Source Pro's can guide you through the implementation of the TRIANGLE, including the selection and training of the marketing and sales staff to strengthen your VISION for the company. You save the time and much of the selection process because the top choices will be screened out of the masses of applicants for you. After selection, the Pros will train and monitor the activities of your new sales people to insure that their activity levels meet or exceed your sales contact goals. Having a marketing outsource Pro on your team monitoring results and coaching the sales people keeps the whole process on track and above board.

You make an investment in the process that makes your commitment to change more likely to succeed. The changes you're making get a jump-start and you concentrate on your core competence of producing high quality installations. And here's the BONUS. When the process is complete and you're up and running in a completely new and profitable direction, you have gained all of the insight and expertise that you need to continue expansion with more products and directions to manage your sales people as you grow.

Where do you find these professional out source people? There are national firms with "one shot deal" seminars and ongoing consulting packages…but you don't have many peers promoting the huge success they have enjoyed from any "out of the industry" training. Ideally you need insight and a fast track to leap to the next level, but general one day training seminars seldom provides the catalyst you need. That means, you may need more than just a good education, you need implementation!

Here comes the shameless self promotion part. The difference we make is that we can be there to help you create the plan and then implement the plan for you, not just tell you what you should do! **You will find our contact information on page 209 .** Call us and we will tell you how we can work together to make your reactive business into a proactive sales and marketing powerhouse!

Our final words regarding all of the things that we have mentioned in this book are to hope that what we have offered to you has been useful. We also hope that our book related to the subject of your business profits should at least offer some ideas that you may not have thought about doing.

We think that your market position advantage by adopting some of our recommendations can materialize very quickly, in some cases, depending on how many best practices are part of your company culture. And some will take a while to achieve.

Please remember, that everything that we offered to you may not be cost effective or otherwise appropriate to your business type or environment. The items that are "low hanging fruit" are the best practices that often have little cost and maximum positive benefit such as taking care of your employees through good training, supervision and encouragement.

Bill Wise CPP is a Certified Protection Professional and President of Security Wise Group LLC®. Prior to founding SWG® in 2004, he worked for over 26 years as a security executive for large retail companies. His experience ranges from directing security and safety operations at hotel and convention complexes to the position of Regional Loss Prevention Manager for a Fortune 500 company for 14 years where he developed successful loss prevention strategies, policies, procedures and products. He is active in professional organizations as a Vice President for the Eastern States Criminal Investigators Association, a member of the American Society for Industrial Security, a member of the American Society of Safety Engineers and is certified by the Pennsylvania State Self Insurance Program.

Bill is also the author of **"Competitive Advantage-Fixing Small Business Security And Safety Problems"** , Second Edition published 9/2007.

Joey Dalessio is a Business Development Executive who has been marketing, developing, and managing security industry businesses since 1973. His career started in the family physical security business, working his way up from bench and field technician to general manager, learning product, operations and account management expertise. He then moved into hardware manufacturing as the national sales manager for a door and frame accessory company followed by positions as national sales manager, VP-Sales and VP-GM for the leading high security company in North America, building key and access control processes, procedures and programs.

As an independent outsource Business Development Manager, Joey has successfully built an improved capability nationwide network of security professionals, implemented marketing & sales, operations and financial infrastructure programs in wholesale distribution and developed target marketing and sales programs for manufacturers of mechanical and electronic security products.

Joey is the Director. Business Development for Marks USA a full service manufacturer of locksets for Commercial, Industrial, Educational, Government and Healthcare Facilities. Marks USA headquarters and manufacturing plant are located in Amityville, New York.

Illustrations in this book were created by **Danny deBruin** who is a cartoonist and graphic artist. He holds a masters degree in education and is completing a second masters. His work has appeared in Newsday, Cracked Magazine, the Long Island Voice, Howard Stern's book, Private Parts, the Long Islander, and a number of other publications.

For more information, see www.dannydebruin.com.

For Daryl the search is over... He's a man with a plan!

What We Do At Security Wise Group LLC®

Loss of profits due to theft, waste, poor safety practices and bad accounting procedures can be found in every company. These losses mean that our customers are working harder for a smaller share of the return on their investment!

What our customers get to keep is what we are all about. Most large companies employ Loss Prevention Managers to help reduce shrinkage of cash, inventory and other assets. Loss Prevention Managers reduce employee theft, Workers Compensation costs, ensure compliance with company rules and procedures and help more profits flow through to the bottom line. Large companies pay, on average, over 1/2 % of gross sales for security hardware and loss prevention personnel. Small to medium sized companies simply cannot afford to spend this level of capitalization and labor cost.

At Security Wise Group LLC® we have assembled loss prevention and business development professionals that can provide security systems through our partner companies and procedures to combat losses that really work and are cost effective.

We become "Your Loss Prevention Department™" for our end user commercial customers by providing an ongoing service that addresses the need to establish standards and procedures that reduce the opportunity for losses. And the service is affordable because you pay for the services that you need, when you need it!

How does it work? We evaluate potential for loss using a custom-designed security systems audit that is modeled on the latest published standards. We zero in on the systems that our customers need to effectively control losses. It's all about people and procedures to improve profit margin. Our Loss Prevention and Hardware Survey evaluation provides the systems, procedures and equipment recommendations our customers need to reduce losses and an available on-going reevaluation process to help make sure that the system is working.

The initial survey and evaluation is typically provide without charge to our commercial end user customer! We provide them with ongoing assistance with the selection of loss barriers such as safes, alarms and the latest digital CCTV systems. Our Board Certified CPP Loss Prevention and Business Development Professionals help sort through solutions that make sense for our particular customers needs. And, most importantly, we are available as an ongoing solution for problems.

Affordable loss prevention services are now available to all companies regardless of size!

How to find us:

If you would like information on how you can bring SWG® services to you or your clients contact:

Bill Wise CPP at 267-994-0024

Joey Dalessio at 717-519-0579

E-mail at:

bill@securitywisegroup.com

joeyd@securitywisegroup.com

Visit SWG® on the web at http://www.securitywisegroup.com

Check out:

- Our seminars

- Our ongoing services for our customers and security hardware dealers

- Business Development Marketing Planning and Plan Execution

- Event participation speakers and book signing events.

- Newsletter service "Security Searchlight"

- End user customer consulting services

- Our book publications

  AND More!

At Security Wise Group LLC®, we offer a number of tools for you to improve communications with your customers. You can check it out on line and download a sample page or call us at the listed numbers!

http://www.securitywisegroup.com

Security Searchlight Subscription Menu

The price for the Security Searchlight Newsletter is based on an annual subscription price for 4 issues. The basic 4-page edition will have the subscribers Name/Logo on the title and Name/Logo along with contact info on the last page mail label section.

Security Searchlight

Available in two versions. *"Security Searchlight"* for commercial customers and *"Security Searchlight At Home"* for residential customers. Subscriptions commence with receipt of payment, which triggers the first current issue and 3 subsequent issues at the advertised quarterly completion dates. Subscribers are licensed to use the material in E-mail or printed formats. We do all the work, incorporate your company name and logo and you get the credit!

Pay for your subscription by credit card by going to the following link!

The link for more information and payment is:
http://www.securitywisegroup.com/securitysearchlight.html

Contact:
Joey Dalessio: joeyd@securitywisegroup.com
Bill Wise CPP: bill@securitywisegroup.com

Security Wise Group LLC
123 Harrison Ave.
Morrisville, PA 19067
267-994-0024

In addition to the basic 4-page custom editions, the subscriber can also opt for:

1. Subscribe to both editions!

2. A Custom 2 page insert option is available for special events or promotions. Price is negotiated depending on the amount of artwork and work to create.

3. A fully customized 4 page newsletter with custom title artwork is available with your products exclusively. Call us for details!

4. Subscription rates are also available at a reduced price without personalized logos and addresses. See our website or call!

Security Searchlight At Home

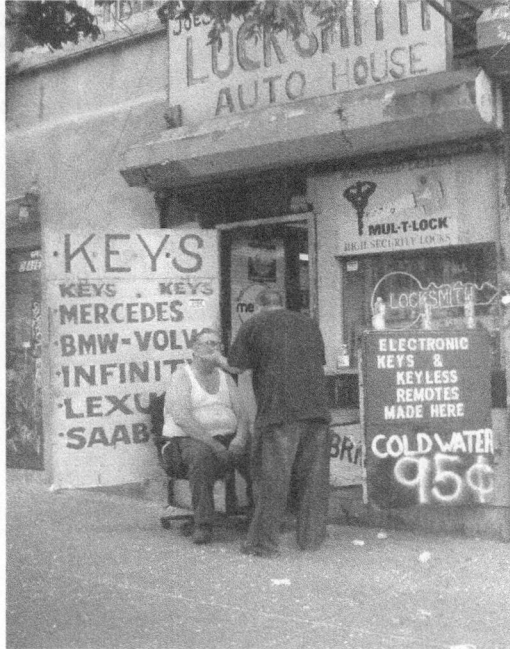

Meanwhile down at Joe's,
it's casual Friday and the
price of water is up!

And finally Daryl says: "When you cross the bridge and transition into a Proactive Marketing and Sales Business, all sorts of new directions are possible!"

www.ingramcontent.com/pod-product-compliance
Lightning Source LLC
Chambersburg PA
CBHW022056210326
41519CB00054B/469